French Crash Course:

A No-BS, Seven-Day Guide to Learning Basic French (with audio)

Important ! The link to download the MP3 is available at the end of this book.

Table of Contents

Introduction

Faster is not always better... *or is it?*

Everyone is crazy about everything fast and instant these days. Fast cars, fast food, instant dinners, instant dates... and the list goes on. I do not want to be that archaic voice in your head telling you "all good things take time." But, really, they do, just like falling in love, cooking a perfect dish, and learning a language like French.

Learning French takes time. Learning French is not like instant food. It is a Ratatouille or a Bouillabaisse that needs to be cooked low and slow for it to turn out deliciously well. However, while this is definitely a preferred approach to learning French, and one I firmly believe in, I also understand that *slow* is just not an option in some cases.

Whether you like it or not, sometimes learning at a slow pace is just not in the cards for you. So, you need a book that can teach French very quickly.

For when slow is not an option....

Congratulations! You have officially found that one book. This is "it". You have stumbled upon an awesome teaching tool that knows exactly what you need **right now**.

But before we continue, let me set the record straight: there is no way you can master French in just seven days.

Let that sink in for a moment.

I can imagine a lot of raised eyebrows and a smattering of *what-is-this-guy-talking-about* or *wait-you-gotta-be-kidding-me* looks right about now. But we need to be realistic about this process.

I have no intentions of giving you false hope and over-promising that you can be fluent in French in just a few days. Unless, of course, you are a language savant like Daniel Tammet, who can become fluent in any language within the span of a week. Or if you have magic beans. Or a language super-gene. Which is kind of the same thing, I think.

So, wait... *What is this book really all about then?*

We have established that this book is not like one of those get-rich-quick/ lose-weight-fast/learn-French-in-a-few-days hoax-type things you often come across.

What this book aims to do is:

- speed things up a little by compressing basic French language instruction with immersion techniques giving you seven days of highly substantial French lessons.

- guide you through the whole process by providing you with **FREE audio** material to help you speak and pronounce French words, not just quickly, but properly as well. Improve your listening comprehension skills with the ONLY book of its kind that offers free audio at a low-price point.

- provide seven days of high-impact French language lessons grouped into easy-to-follow daily topics, exercises, and fun activities that include: *Le Film du Jour* (Film of the Day), *La Musique du Jour* (Music of the Day), and *L'activité du Jour* (Activity of the Day).

- build a stable starting point for learners who want to begin strong when learning French.

- equip you with all the essentials you need to be able to form a basic grasp of the French language and arm you with enough know-how to help you get by in a French-speaking environment.

While I am not promising that you will be a whiz at French in seven days, I can promise that you will learn all the basics of the French language FASTER and in a more immersive way. Merge your language lessons with fun activities like watching French movies, listening to French music, and more, all with the help of free supplementary audio that you can listen to anywhere.

So, is this *that one book* -- the game-changer that totally gets you?

To find out, check all that apply:

You are:

- an impatient human being who cannot take months of lessons in order to learn French.

- traveling for an extended period of time (or moving) to a French-speaking destination and you want to make sure you will survive and thrive in your new environment.

- officially on a hiatus from life in general and wish to spend a full week learning something new.
- planning an entire week of self-improvement, and learning French is on your checklist.
- an employee or businessman who needs to learn the basics of French quickly for something career-related.
- an especially competitive student who wants to make headway in learning French in order to leave a trail of dust in your opponents' – *er, classmates'* – awestruck faces as you happily speed past them in French class.
- not into long language learning processes. Your attention wanders or motivation lags in the long term.
- a strong believer that faster is always better.
- someone who studied French a long time ago (e.g. in high school), and just want to refresh your memory a bit.
- going to France very soon and just want to enjoy your holiday by being able to speak the language.

If you checked at least one of the above, then this book is written with you in mind.

If you're ready, as I am sure you are, buckle up and hold on tight for an entire week of fun and fast French lessons that you will surely enjoy!

Merci.

Frédéric BIBARD

Founder, Talk in French.com

Chapter 1 - Day 1
The essentials of basic communication

Today, we will learn all the essentials of basic communication.

La Prononciation: Pronunciation

Alright, no need to panic. French pronunciation can seem like one of the scariest and overwhelming aspects of the language, but have no fear! Once you get the basics down, pronunciation anxiety will be a thing of the past.

The first thing to consider is that the French alphabet uses the same basic Latin alphabet we use. That means we use the same twenty-six letters, the same A, E, I, O, U, and Y vowels, and the same twenty consonants. Considering the sheer magnitude of sounds found in a variety of other languages -- this should give you cause to stop biting those nails! French is very kind in this area.

Les Voyelles: Vowels

Vowels are sounds that are pronounced through the mouth (with the exception of nasal vowels) without obstructing the lips, tongue, or throat.

For **les voyelles**, or French vowels, there are a few things to keep in mind:

- Most French vowels situate themselves further forward in the mouth than English vowels.
- It is very important that you keep your tongue taut as you pronounce each vowel.

Les Consonnes: Consonants

For **les consonnes,** many of the sounds are very similar to those found in English, which is another cause for celebration!

The following set of charts is an overview of all the sounds found in the French language. This is more of a list to refer to than something to memorize right away.

Les Lettres Simples (Simple Letters)

Listen Track 1:

French letters	Sounds like	English examples	French examples
A	A	r[a]t	bras (arm) chat (cat)
B	B	[b]utter	bateau (boat) bébé (baby)
C before O, A, U	K	[c]andy	carte (map) col (collar)
C before E, I, Y	S	[s]tanza	citron (lemon) ciment (cement)
Ç	S	[s]ilence	ça (this) garçon (boy)
D	D	[d]og	dos (back) dans (in)
e	U	b[u]bble	le (the) ce (this)
F	F	[f]ood	faire (to make) fleur (flower)
G before O, A, U	G	[g]row	gauche (left) guerre (war)
G before E, I, Y	J	dé[j]à vu	orange (orange) girafe (giraffe)
H	always silent	--	hibou (owl) hache (ax)
I	Ee	f[ee]t	bisou (kiss) cri (shout)
J	J	dé[j]à vu	je (I) jamais (never)
K	K	[k]oala	képi (kepi) koala (koala)
I	L	[l]ove	lapin (rabbit) livre (book)
M	M	[m]other	maman (mom) mon (mine)
N	N	[n]ever	non (no) nid (nest)
O	O	z[o]rro	domino (domino) collègue (colleague)

P	P	[p]asta	papa (dad) patate (potato)
Q	Q	[c]ap	quatre (four) qui (who)
R	R	a[r]t deco	rare (unusual) radis (radish)
S	S	[s]nail	son (sound) savoir (know)
T	T	[t]ag	tata (auntie) ton (your)
U	ew	déjà v[u]	tu (you) ruban (ribbon)
V	V	[v]iew	vivre (to live) venir (to come)
W	V	wa[v]e	Wagon
W (English origin)	W	[w]ater	Whisky wapiti
X, inside a word or when ex- is followed by a consonant or at the end of words	X	e[x]cess	Expert luxe (luxury)
X, at the beginning of a word or when ex- is followed by a vowel or H	X	e[x]am	exemple (example) examen (exam/ test)
X, at the end of words	S	[s]olution	dix (ten) six (six)
X (rare cases)	Z	[z]ero	deuxième (second)
X, at the end of words to indicate plural	Silent	--	choux (cabbages) chevaux (horses)
Y	Y	[y]am	yoyo, yacht
Z	Z	[z]ip	zéro (zero) zèbre (zebra)

Les Sons Complexes (Complex Sounds)

Listen Track 2:

French letters	Sounds like	English examples	French examples
ai	ai	l[ai]ssez-faire	aimer (to love) faire (to do)
-ain, -aim	un	verd[un]	pain (bread) faim (hunger)
au	o	r[o]pe	paume (palm) baume (balm)
ch	sh	[sh]ampoo	château (castle) chapeau (hat)
ei	e	m[e]n	peine (pain) reine (queen)
eu	e	th[e]	peu (little) deux (two)
-er, -ez	a	d[a]y	manger (to eat) vous allez (you go)
eau, -aud, -ot	o	[o]zone	râteau (rake) chaud (hot) pot (jar)
em, en before consonant	en	[en]core	entre (between) emploi (job)
ha-	a	r[a]t	habiter (to live)
ill	y	[y]ogurt	fille (girl) billet (ticket)
oi	wa	[wa]ter	toit (roof) quoi (what)
oin	oo + un	t[oo]+Verd[un]	loin (far) coin (corner)
on, om	on	s[on]g	bon (good) chanson (song)
ou	oo	t[wo]	fou (crazy) cou (neck)
ph	f	[f]ather	Phare (lighthouse)
sc before o, a, u	sc	[sc]oundrel	sculpter (to sculpt) scorpion
sc before e, i, y	sc	[sc]enario	scie (saw) scène (stage)
th	t	[t]ime	thym (thyme) thèse (thesis)

ti	s	[s]tone	objection (objection) prophétie (prophecy)
um, un, word ending or before a consonant	un	verd[un]	un (a) parfum (perfume)
ui	wi	ki[wi]	pluie (rain) cuisine (kitchen)

Les Accents

Listen Track 3:

French letters	Sounds like	English examples	French examples
à	a	r[a]t	à (in)
é	a	d[a]y	école (school) café (coffee)
è, ê	e	m[e]n	père (father) mère (mother)
â, î, ô, û pronounced as a, i, o, u			château (castle) hôpital (hospital)
ä, ë, ï, ö, ü, the tréma indicates that the two adjacent vowels must both be pronounced	a i	n[a i]ve	Noël (Christmas) haïr (to hate)

Le Vocabulaire: Vocabulary

Today, we will stick with what you already know. Thanks to the Norman conquest of 1066, 10,000 words were introduced into the English language, and about three-fourths of those words are still part of your daily vernacular. That, paired with the fact that both French and English shared some Latin/Greek root words, means that there are a ton of words that English-speakers currently share with their French friends.

For example, take the word *auditorium,* which has the same spelling and similar pronunciation in both French and English. The Latin *aud,* meaning *hear*, is the root of that word. The same goes for the Greek *astir*, meaning "star", and *astrology* (**astrologie** in French).

This brings us to the concept of cognates and false cognates, or **vrais amis** and **faux amis**, respectively.

Vrais amis

The literal translation of **vrais amis** is "true friends," which is exactly how you will feel when you use them. They are friendly words that have the exact same spelling and meaning in both French and English. They are the free gift bag of vocabulary words that will act as a foundational cushion as you embark on your French journey.

However, French true cognates are oftentimes pronounced differently than their English twins. This is actually a blessing in disguise! Knowing the English pronunciation will help you comprehend and internalize the French pronunciation of the same word. There are over 1,700 French cognates, so a basic understanding of pronunciation will make all of those words available to you, which will then give context to words and phrases you do not yet understand.

For example, let's look at this sentence:

Ce week-end, je vais aller au concert jazz avec ma classe.

What looks familiar? We have *week-end*, *concert*, *jazz*, and potentially *classe*. From this, it is not that hard to put the sentence into context:

This weekend, I'm going to a jazz concert with my class.

Simple, right? And, like *classe*, there are plenty of other words that are near-cognates, or words with almost the same spelling and the exact same meaning. They will become fast friends for you as well. Here is a list of common cognates:

Useful words at work:

Listen Track 4:

absence (feminine noun)

accident (masculine)

client (masculine)

collaboration (feminine)

communication (feminine)

contact (masculine)

document (masculine)

fax (masculine)

message (masculine)

mission (feminine)

obligation (feminine)

payable (adjective)

profession (feminine)

solution (feminine)

test (masculine)

Planning your weekend get-away:

Listen Track 5:

barbecue (masculine)

bikini (masculine)

bistro (masculine)

bungalow (masculine)

camp (masculine)

casino (masculine)

concert (masculine)

kayak (masculine noun)

parachute (masculine)

parasol (masculine)

promenade (feminine)

ski (masculine)

sport (masculine)

taxi (masculine)

tennis (masculine)

valise (feminine)

zoo (masculine)

At the restaurant:

Listen Track 6:

addition (feminine)

apéritif (masculine)

chef (masculine)

dessert (masculine)

entrée (feminine)

fruit (masculine)

gourmet (masculine)

hors-d'oeuvre (masculine)

menu (masculine)

pizza (feminine)

quiche (feminine)

sorbet (masculine)

steak (masculine)

vodka (feminine)

Faux-Amis

The literal translation of **faux-amis** is "false friend." These words have the same spelling as their English counterparts, but do not let that trick you into thinking they have the same meaning. It is very easy to use these words with confidence in a French-speaking situation, only to find yourself misunderstood or embarrassed when a French-speaker does not have any idea what you are talking about.

For instance, an English-speaking friend of mine was absolutely mortified when she discovered at the end of her first semester that "je suis excitée!" did not mean "I am excited!" in the way she understood it in English. It was only after her professor realized this had become the student's go-to phrase that she kindly informed her what she had really been saying all along:

"I am turned on!" At that moment, she really wished she had not assumed it was a cognate and took the extra couple of minutes to look it up.

The confusion can come from the English-speaker's side of things as well. It would be confusing if someone asked you what "robe" you are planning to wear to the party, when "robe" in French means "dress."

The main suggestion for avoiding these embarrassing blunders is to study your false cognates well. Once you know them and the proper French word to use instead, you will avoid a large chunk of beginner mistakes.

La Grammaire: Grammar

Sentence Structure

French sentence structure is very similar to English. There are exceptions to this rule, but the general sentence formula is this:

NOUN or PRONOUN + VERB + ADJECTIVE or ADVERB

When taking on the task of creating your own sentences, try to label them to ensure you are following the proper structure.

[N]   [V]   [ADJ]

[Le chien] [est] [adorable]. = The dog is adorable.

[P]   [V]   [ADV]

[Je] [chante] [doucement]. = I sing softly.

In order to find success with this formula, it is necessary to understand how nouns, pronouns, verbs, adjectives, and adverbs work in French.

Les noms: Nouns

When learning French nouns, there are a few things to remember:

1. **Every noun has a gender.** This is the biggest distinction from English. Each noun can be feminine or masculine.
2. **Every noun has an article preceding it.** For our current purposes, this will be the French form of *the*, or **le** (masculine), **la** (feminine), and **les** (plural) (with the exceptions of a few, such as: Internet).

3. **Every noun can be either singular or plural.** When learning French, we refer to this as the number.

4. **There is no rhyme or reason to assigning gender.** There is no trick to assigning gender to nouns. It is very important to memorize the article with each noun, just as though it is part of the word itself.

Les articles: French Articles

In English, articles are typically *the* or *a*. In French, the articles **le, la,** and **les** (the) are called definite articles, or **les articles définis.** The articles **un, une,** and **des** are known as **les articles indéfinis,** or indefinite articles.

Singular masculine articles:

le (the) and **un** (a).

Singular feminine articles:

la (the) and **une** (a).

Plural masculine and feminine articles:

les (the) and **des** (some).

Example:

Listen Track 7:

La fille = the girl (feminine definite article)
Une fille = a girl (feminine indefinite article)
Les filles = the girls (plural feminine definite article)
Des filles = some girls (plural feminine indefinite article)

Note: the plural form means that you must add an extra "s" to the end of the noun. It is this, paired with the plural article, that denotes the number of the noun.

Les pronoms: Pronouns

Pronouns replace nouns. There are two different types of pronouns in French:

1. **Pronoms personnels (personal pronouns).** These pronouns specifically address a person or subject.

2. **Pronoms impersonnels (impersonal pronouns).** These pronouns do not refer to a person or specific subject.

Example:

Il pleut. It is raining.

In this case, **il** is an impersonal pronoun, as it does not refer to a person or specific subject. Personal pronouns are often used with impersonal nouns, such as *pleuvoir* (to rain).

Note: French pronouns have direct translations with English pronouns.

Les pronoms: Pronouns

Listen Track 8:

Je	I	Mon/Ma	My	Moi	Me
Tu	You	Ton/Ta	Your	Toi	You
Il/Elle	He/She	Son/Sa	His/Her	Lui/Elle	He/She
Nous	We	Notre	Our	Nous	Us
Vous	You (formal)	Votre	Your (formal)	Vous	You (formal)
Ils/Elles	He/She (plural)	Leurs	Their	Eux	Them

Examples:

Listen Track 9:

Je parle anglais. **I** speak English.

Ma sœur est jolie. **My** sister is pretty.

C'est **son** portable. That's **his** cell phone.

Oui, c'est **moi**! Yes, it's **me**!

Les verbes: Verbs

A verb is used to describe an action or the state of the subject noun. The subject can be a noun, as in *le chat* (cat) or a pronoun, as in *il* (it/he).

Some notes about French verbs:

1. **You must conjugate the verb according to the corresponding noun or pronoun.** This is the same in English.

Example:

Le chat est noir. The cat is black.

Le chat is a singular masculine noun. **Est** is the verb **être** (to be) conjugated in the singular form.

Example:

Les chats sont noirs. The cats are black.

Les chats is a plural masculine noun. **Sont** is the verb **être** (to be) conjugated in the plural form.

Now, let's learn some verbs! Note that these are infinitive verbs, which means that we add **to** to the verb, as in **manger** (to eat) and **danser** (to dance).

Popular French Verbs:

Listen Track 10:

Être - (to be)

Avoir - (to have)

Pouvoir - (to be able)

Faire - (to do/make)

Mettre - (to put, place)

Dire - (to say, tell)

Devoir - (to have to)

Prendre - (to take)

Donner - (to give)

Aller - (to go)

Vouloir - (to want)

Savoir - (to know)

Les adjectifs: Adjectives

Adjectives describe nouns. Here are some rules for them in French:

1. **The adjective must match the gender and number of the noun it describes.**

   Example:

   La fille intelligente. The smart girl.

   Fille is a singular feminine noun, and its pronoun is the singular feminine **la**. This means that the adjective *intelligent* must agree in the feminine, so we add **-e** to the end.

   Example:

   Le pantalon bleu. The blue pants.

   Pantalon is a singular masculine noun, and its pronoun is the singular masculine **le**. In this case, the adjective *bleu* must remain in its masculine form.

   Example:

   Des beaux oiseaux. The beautiful birds.

   Oiseaux is a plural masculine noun, and its pronoun is the plural **des**. This means that we must use the adjective *beau* in the masculine plural form, so it becomes *beaux*.

2. **Adjectives can be placed before or after nouns.** A nifty trick for this is that adjectives placed before a noun usually relate to beauty, age, goodness, badness, and size (B.A.G.S).

   Examples:

   Listen Track 11:

   Un jeune homme = a young man

   Une grande femme = a tall woman

   Des bonnes fraises = good strawberries

   Un vieux livre = an old book

Les adverbes: adverbs

An adverb modifies or qualifies a verb, which is a fancy way of saying that they describe the verb it refers to. In English, we do this by taking an adjective and adding **-ly**, as in *slowly, beautifully, cautiously*, etc. In French, adverbs generally operate in the same way by adding **-ment**.

Examples:

Heureusement - happily

Brusquement - abruptly

Lentement - slowly

In a sentence, these verbs come after the verb it describes, as in the **N + V + ADV** formula.

Examples:

Listen Track 12:

Mon grand-père marche fièrement. My grandfather walks proudly.

La porte ferme silencieusement. The door closes silently.

Tu souris sincèrement. You smile genuinely.

La conversation: Speaking

Les salutations: Greetings

It is a special thing to be able to properly greet someone in another language. It is usually the first step when learning, and it can feel so empowering. As you begin this exciting part of your learning experience, try to keep this quote in mind:

"Avoir une autre langue, c'est posséder une deuxième âme"
("To have another language is to possess a second soul»)

Charlemagne

Learning a language gives you an opportunity to explore new sides of yourself you did not know existed. So when you are afraid of pronouncing something wrong or worried how you will be perceived, just think of this as an opportunity to become the French version of you!

These are some French greetings to get you started:

Hellos:

Listen Track 13:

Bonjour - Hello/Good morning/Good afternoon

Salut - Hello (informal)

Bonsoir - Good evening

Bonne nuit - Good night

Goodbyes:

Listen Track 14:

Au revoir - Goodbye

Salut - Goodbye (informal)

Bonne journée - Have a good day

À bientôt - See you soon

À plus tard - See you later

À plus - See you

À demain - See you tomorrow

How are you?

Listen Track 15:

Formal:

Comment allez vous?

Informal:

Ça va?

Comment ça va?

Comment va-tu?

Tu vas bien?

La Réponse Affirmative (Positive response)

Listen Track 16:

Ça va! - I'm well! (informal)

Ça va (très) bien! - I'm (very) well! (standard)

Je vais (très) bien. - I am (very) well, thank you. (formal)

La Réponse Négative (Negative Response)

Listen Track 17:

Ça va pas. - Not well. (informal)

Non, ça ne va pas bien. - No, I'm not well. (standard)

Non, je ne vais pas bien. - No, I am not well. (formal)

Comme ci, comme ça. - I'm so-so.

La Présentation (Introductions)

Listen Track 18:

Je me présente. - Let me introduce myself.

Je m'appelle _____. - My name is _____.

Mon prénom est... - My first name is...

Je suis... - I am...

L'immersion: Immersion

Immersion is crucial to absorbing and retaining a language, so let's make it fun! This week, we will focus on slow, easy to understand movies, music, and media.

Le Film du Jour: Film of the Day

"Être et avoir"

This documentary chronicles the challenges and triumphs of a school teacher working in a one-room school in rural France. The film has received a myriad of awards, and the film's slow-moving progression allows beginners to keep up with the pace. Since this film also provides great insight into the French education system, you will be learning a lot about the French language and methods for learning it.

La Musique du Jour: Music of the Day

Edith Piaf

You have probably heard a lot of Edith Piaf. She is one of the most iconic French singers of all time, and songs like "Non, Je ne Regrette rien" and "La Vie en Rose" are well-loved even in the English-speaking world. This, along with her spectacular enunciation, makes her great for study. Each of her songs are simple and seem to touch on a great grammar point. "Non, Je ne Regrette rien" is an excellent example of this, as she showcases French negation in a variety of ways.

Note: Since she sings in an older style which draws out and elongates her lyrics, it is important to note that her style of speech is primarily for picking out nuances in pronunciation. Modern singers we will encounter in the coming days will adopt a more shortened style of pronunciation.

L'activité du Jour: Activity of the Day

La Bande Dessinée (Comic Books)

Comic books are a *huge* deal in France. Known as "the ninth art," French bande dessinée, or BDs for short, they are definitely not just for kids and teens.

The most famous BDs come from both France and Belgium (another says francophone, or French-speaking country), including but not limited to "Astérix," "Tintin," "Lucky Luke," and "Spirou". These stories have cultural significance, bite-size dialog and grammar points, and wide appeal. It will also be a great conversation topic when you go to France!

Even if some of the language is too elevated for your current level, you will be able to glean context from the images along with it. These BDs are heavy on the history, but that only serves to heighten your knowledge of intellectual French vocabulary in a fun, engaging way. So have fun!

Chapter 2 - Day 2
Perfect your pronunciation

Today, we will perfect our pronunciation of French accents, round out our knowledge of French articles, and learn some vocabulary for getting around.

La Prononciation: Pronunciation

Les accents: French accents

French uses five diacritical marks (or accents). They are absolutely essential for proper pronunciation, and being able to pick them out in writing is crucial.

Listen Track 19:

´ - accent aigu (occurs only above the letter e)..............**répétez** (repeat)

` - accent grave..**très** (very)

^ - accent circonflexe...**île** (island)

ç - cedille (occurs only on the letter c).......................**ça va?** (how are you?)

¨ - tréma ....**haïr** (to hate)

Note: Except for the **cédille**, or cedilla, on the capital letter **c**, accents are not typically used on capital letters.

L'accent aigu: Acute accent

The acute accent only appears above the letter **e** and is used to change the **e** sound to **ay** (as in *bay*). It often specifies that an **s** used to follow that vowel in the original Latin. It is the most common of the accents, so most learners of the language find this one to be the easiest to pick up.

Examples:

Listen Track 20:

- **marché** (*mar-shay*, meaning market)
- **médecin** (*may-deh-sehn*, meaning doctor)

- **école** (*ay-cole*, meaning school)
- **méchant** (*may-shant*, meaning mean, i.e., a mean person)
- **café** (*cah-fay*, meaning coffee)

L'accent grave

It is placed over **e** to indicate that the next syllable is silent. It makes the e sound like **ea** (*pear*). It can also be found over **a** and **u** for a handful of words, and is usually used to distinguish between words that would be homographs otherwise, as in **ou** (or) and **où** (where).

Examples:

Listen Track 21:

- **deuxième** (*doozy-em*, meaning second)
- **père** (*pare*, meaning father)
- **secrète** (*say-kret*, meaning secret)
- **frère** (*fruh-air*, meaning brother)
- **suède** (*soo-ed*, meaning Sweden)

L'accent circonflexe: Curcumflex Accent

The circumflex, also affectionately referred to as "the hat," has absolutely no bearing on pronunciation. Many French people who support reform of the language have been petitioning to have the accent removed from the language entirely. Originally used in old French to indicate the lost "s" that existed in the Latin version of a word, it is one of those grammatical quirks that has carried on throughout the centuries. English, too, carries a similar quirk, as the same words that carry this Latin ancestry still carry that **s**.

Just like the **l'accent grave**, it also functions to distinguish between words that would be homographs, as in **du** (contraction for de + le) and **dû** (the past participle of devoir).

There are not many words that have the circumflex. That being said, they are still an important facet of the language, and it is important to know what to do with them when you see them.

Examples:

Listen Track 22:

- **honnête** (*on-ette*, meaning honest)
- **hôpital** (*o-pee-tal*, meaning hospital)
- **forêt** (*for-ay*, meaning forest)
- **hôtel** (*owe-tel*, meaning hotel)
- **âge** (*ah-zjuh*, meaning age)

La Cédile: Cedilla

The cedilla is only found under the letter **c**. Its purpose is to transform a hard **c** (like the **k** sound in *card*) into a soft **c** (like the **s** sound in *cereal*). Because of this, the cedilla is never found in front of an **e** or **i**, as a **c** always carries the soft **c** sound in front of these vowels.

Examples:

Listen Track 23:

- **garçon** (*gahr-sohn*, meaning "boy)
- **français** (*frahn-say*, meaning French or the French language**)**
- **leçon** (*ley-sohn*, meaning lesson)
- **ça** (*sah*, meaning that)
- **reçu** (*reh-sue*, meaning received)

Le Tréma: Dieresis

The dieresis, also called an *umlaut*, can only be found when two vowels are next to each other. This indicates that both vowels must be pronounced separately.

Examples:

Listen Track 24:

- **Noël** (*no-elle*, meaning Christmas)
- **Héroïne** (*err-oh-een*, meaning heroine)
- **naïve** (*nigh-eve*, meaning naïve)

- **coïncidence** (*ko-ehn-see-dahns*, meaning coincidence)
- **Jamaïque** (*jam-eh-eek*, meaning Jamaica)

Remember, it is incredibly important to use accents properly when learning French. Not knowing what they mean can impede your pronunciation, and missing one in a word is the same thing as misspelling that word. Just like remembering whether to use **le** or **la** for each new vocabulary word you learn, treat accents like they are crucial accessories on the words you are learning. You would not forget your pants or shirt, so be kind to your French vocabulary and make sure they are dressed to impress. If you pay close attention to them, you will be pronouncing (and writing) like a pro.

Le Vocabulaire: Vocabulary

Franglais: English Loan Words

Bouncing off of yesterday's *vrais amis et faux-amis*, today we will touch on some modern English words that have influenced the French language. Due to the fact that English is gaining popularity as a global business language, France has adopted many vocabulary words from it. Globalization has also made it popular to use English words and phrases in everyday conversation.

It is exceedingly important to note that these loan words are often pronounced and utilized differently in French. So, in order to avoid experiencing embarrassing conversations, be sure to know exactly what the word means in French before using it.

Culturally, France is very proud of its language. There is even an organization dating back to 1635 called L'Académie Française, which continues to regulate and maintain the "purity" of the language. These days, the forty peer-elected members, known as Les Quarante (the forty) or Les Immortels (the immortals), often focus on the task of reducing the influx of English loan words by choosing or creating French equivalents. An example of this is the 2011 decision to replace the word *e-mail* with *courriel*. The decision sparked a lot of debate which rages on today.

This is important to acknowledge for a couple of reasons. First, although English loan words are a growing trend in France, there are still some people (especially of the older generation) who view these words as a faux-pas. In respect-driven situations, it might be best to avoid these terms (unless you hear the other person use them, of course). Another thing to acknowledge is that the newer generation and contemporary media outlets in France absolutely adore using English terms, even if there are obvious traditional French equivalents. Terms like "super cool," "hyper-sexy," and "le top du top" (top of the top) are used often, but should be considered in the same light as our own slang terms.

All in all, these terms are certified to make your French sound relaxed and conversational. In a business environment, using these terms with proper pronunciation will be sure to create a great impression. As long as you know when and how to use them, they are another easy way to make your French "super bon."

Common Franglais Terms

Everyday words:

Listen Track 25:

baby-foot: table football

basket: sports shoe, basketball

brushing: blow-dry

camping: campsite

dressing: walk-in closet

catch: wrestling

flipper: pinball machine

footing: jogging

forcing: pressure

jogging: tracksuit

lifting: face-lift

people: celebrity

planning: schedule

pressing: dry-cleaner

relooking: make-over

smoking: tuxedo

sweat: sweatshirt

warning: hazard lights

parking: parking lot

planning: schedule

zapping: channel hopping

station-service: service station

Verbs

Listen Track 26:

bruncher: to have brunch

googeliser: to Google

Skyper: to Skype

tweeter: to tweet

liker: to like

follower: to follow (on Twitter)

La Grammaire: Grammar

Les articles: French Articles

You learned the basic French articles yesterday, so today we will build upon that more.

Review:

In English, the typical articles are **the** or **a**. In French, the articles **le**, **la**, and **les** (the) are called definite articles, or **les articles définis**. The articles **un**, **une**, and **des** are known as **les articles indéfinis**, or indefinite articles.

Singular masculine articles:

le (the) and **un** (a).

Singular feminine articles:

la (the) and **une** (a).

Plural masculine and feminine articles:

les (the) and **des** (some).

Example:

Listen Track 27:

La fille = the girl (feminine definite article)
Une fille = a girl (feminine indefinite article)
Les filles = the girls (plural feminine definite article)
Des filles = some girls (plural feminine indefinite article)

Note: the plural form means that you must add an extra **s** to the end of the noun. It is this paired with the plural article that denotes the number of the noun.

We are going to add a new type of article to the list today.

Les articles partitifs

Les articles partitifs, or partitive articles, are most closely related to *some* or *any* in English. Oftentimes used in relation to food or drink, the partitive article indicates an unknown quantity of something. This can be tricky for

English-speakers, mostly because we largely ignore our use (or lack of use) of the partitive articles. "I bought cheese" would always be sufficient for English, but in French you must say "I bought (some) cheese," or "**J'achète du fromage**." There are four different forms that can be used based on number and gender:

1. "**du**" (masculine)
2. "**de la**" (feminine)
3. "**de l'**" (masculine or feminine, used in front of a vowel or silent **h**)
4. "**des**" (masculine or feminine plural)

To figure out which one to use, keep the noun's number, gender, and first letter in mind:

1. If the noun is singular <u>and</u> starts with a silent vowel or h (known as an **h muet**), use **de l'**.
2. If the noun is plural, use **des.**
3. If the noun is singular or starts with a consonant or **aspirate h** (known as an **h aspire**), use **du** for the masculine noun and **de la** for the feminine noun.

Example:

Je mange de la glace. I'm eating (some) ice cream.

La glace (ice cream) is feminine, and since this person is not indicating they are eating *an* ice cream cone (or denoting a specific number of ice cream cones), **de la** is necessary.

Example:

Ils achètent du poisson. They bought (some) fish.

Poisson (fish) is masculine, so here we use **du** to indicate that (some) indefinite number of fish are being bought.

Example:

Je bois de l'eau. I'm drinking (some) water.

Eau (water) is feminine, and since this noun starts with an **e**, **de l'** is the appropriate article.

Example:

Je mange des petits pois. I'm eating (some) peas.

Petits pois (peas) is a masculine plural, so we use **des** to indicate that you ate (some) peas.

Note: When the quantity is unknown or uncountable, use the partitive article. When the quantity is known or countable, use the indefinite article (or the number of whatever it is you are counting).

Example:

Je mange du pamplemousse. I'm eating (some) grapefruit.

Je mange un pamplemousse. I'm eating a (one) grapefruit.

La négation: Negation

Okay, so now that we have gotten the articles down, we must now remember some exceptions. Negation of articles is easy to remember if you keep this in mind:

Indefinite Articles and Partitive Articles = NE + VERB + PAS DE + NOUN

Definite articles do not follow this, so all you have to do is add the negation form of **ne + verb + pas** and add your definite article.

Example:

J'aime la pizza. I like pizza.

Je n'aime pas la pizza. I don't like pizza.

Since **la** is a definite article, all we have to do is sandwich **ne + pas** in between the verb **aimer.**

Example:

Je mange de la pizza. I eat pizza.

Je ne mange pas de pizza. I don't eat pizza.

Because "I eat pizza" does not indicate a definite amount, we use the feminine partitive article **de la** in this instance. The partitive article makes the **pas...de** exception in the negation form, so we would use **pas de pizza** instead of the incorrect **pas de la pizza**.

Example:

J'achète un gâteau. I'm buying a cake.

Je n'achète pas de gâteau. I'm not buying (any) cake.

The masculine indefinite article **un** is utilized here. Indefinite articles follow the **pas...de** exception for negation, so we would use **pas de gâteau** to indicate that the person is not buying cake.

Reference the chart below to keep in mind how to properly use articles and negation exceptions.

Les articles

Listen Track 28:

Definite Articles	Partitive Articles	Indefinite Articles
J'aime le kiwi. Je n'aime pas le kiwi.	Je mange du kiwi. Je ne mange pas de kiwi.	J'achète un kiwi. Je n'achète pas de kiwi.
J'aime la pomme. Je n'aime pas la pomme.	Je mange de la pomme. Je ne mange pas de pomme.	J'achète une pomme. Je n'achète pas de pomme.
J'aime l'ananas. Je n'aime pas l'ananas.	Je mange de l'ananas. Je ne mange pas d'ananas.	J'achète un ananas. Je n'achète pas d'ananas.
J'aime les fraises. Je n'aime pas les fraises.	Je mange des fraises. Je ne mange pas de fraises.	J'achète des fraises. Je n'achète pas de fraises.

La Conversation: Speaking

Les banalités: Small Talk

Now that you know how to greet someone and introduce yourself, it is time to learn some small talk! Today, we are going to cover some common questions that will come up in introductory conversations, like where someone is from and their nationality. An easy way to keep a conversation going is to memorize these questions/statements; that gets the job done, even if you do not have a good grasp of the ins and outs of French grammar just yet.

Note: Some words have brackets, which indicate the translation for a woman. They are usually pronounced by elongating the **e**. In the case of the **ne**, it is pronounced like **en**, as in *been*.

Where you're from:

Listen Track 29:

D'où êtes-vous? - Where are you from? (formal)

D'où venez-vous? - Where do you come from? (formal)

Où habitez-vous? - Where do you live? (formal)

Tu es d'où? - Where are you from? (familiar)

Tu viens d'où? - Where do you come from? (familiar)

Où est-ce que tu habites? - Where do you live? (familiar)

Où habites-tu? - Where do you live? (familiar)

Je suis (originaire) de (+ ville) - I am (originally) from (+ city)

Je viens de (+ ville) - I come from (+ city)

J'habite à (+ ville) - I live in (+ city)

Ma ville natale est… - My hometown is…

Age/Marital Status:

Listen Track 30:

J'ai...ans. – I am...years old.

Je suis célibataire (marié[e]) - I am single (married)

Nationality:

Listen Track 31:

Je suis...(+ nationalité) - I am (+ nationality)

africain(e) – African

allemand(e) – German

américain(e) - American

anglais(e) – English

australien(ne) – Australian

belge – Belgian

canadien(ne) – Canadian

chinois(e) – Chinese

égyptien(ne) – Egyptian

espagnol(e) – Spanish

français(e) – French

indien(ne) – Indian

irlandais(e) – Irish

italien(ne) – Italian

japonais(e) – Japanese

marocain(e) – Moroccan

mexicain(e) – Mexican

néerlandais(e) – Dutch

polonais(e) – Polish

portugais(e) – Portuguese

russe – Russian

sénégalais(e) – Senegalese

suédois(e) – Swedish

suisse – Swiss

L'Immersion: Immersion

Today is all about keeping up with current French culture. We will also be recapping some of the other points we have learned today, like introductions and articles.

Le film du Jour: Film of the Day

"Amélie (Le fabuleux destin d'Amélie Poulain)"

One of the most well-known French films in contemporary cinema, this film is about the whimsical adventures of a young woman who decides to change the world by discretely helping those around her. Quirky and whimsical, the film is a great introduction to French culture and some slang terms. There are also a lot of introductions going on, which is a nice perk. Its pacing is quick, but most of the dialog is crisp and clear, especially the narration.

La musique du jour: Music of the Day

Emilie Simon

Drawing comparisons from Bjork and Kate Bush, this French singer, songwriter, and composer is an avant-garde marvel. Her down-tempo style is great for relaxation, and her voice is as crisp and clear as can be. She has won a multitude of awards, has been featured in numerous films, and sings in English as well as her native French. She was even tasked with the honor of creating the soundtrack for the French version of March of the Penguins, so her relevance in the modern French music scene is apparent. She is known for songs like "Desert," "Jetaimejetaimejetaime," and her newest single, "Menteur."

L'activité du jour: Activity of the Day

Faire Une Recette: Make a Recipe

Cooking can be a genuinely fun way to learn a language, so why not try your hand at a French recipe...in French! This is an excellent way to continue working on those articles we have been learning today. You will also be gaining some great food vocabulary as well.

Sites like Marmiton or Elle à Table give you the opportunity to find thousands of recipes with the click of a mouse. Of course, these recipes will be using the metric system of measurement, so it is worth it to get friendly with a conversion website as well. Grams and milliliters will quickly become familiar with a little practice. Remember: volume and weight are not the same for every ingredient, so 100 grams of flour and 100 grams of sugar will have very different volume measures in cups.

In order to get the most out of this activity, you will need to whip out your French dictionary. Try to use it as much as possible to translate words you do not know (this is your second day, so that means most of them!), and be sure to write down the translated words you learn for reference. The act of actually searching for a word in a physical dictionary makes it stick so much better than the instant gratification of translation software, so try not to cheat on this one.

A few ingredients common to French grocery stores are quite difficult to track down elsewhere. Recipes that call for "fromage blanc" or "fromage frais" can usually be made with either Greek yogurt or sour cream. "Feuilles de brick" (thin sheets of dough) can easily be replaced by using phyllo dough.

Especially since cuisine is such an integral part of French life, this exercise is just as much a cultural lesson as it is one of grammar and vocabulary. If you are looking for some quintessentially French dishes to try, search for some of the following:

Main Dishes:

Listen Track 32:

- Coq au Vin
- Croque-Monsieur

- Quiche
- Ratatouille
- Bœuf Bourguignon
- Cassoulet
- Moules Frites
- Soupe à l'Oignon

Desserts:

Listen Track 33:

- Madeleines
- Crème brûlée
- Crêpes
- Profiteroles
- Mousse au Chocolat
- Éclair
- Mille Feuilles
- Tarte Tatin

Note: Instructions for French recipes are almost always written in the infinitive, or base, verb form. It is a nice little introduction to some French verbs and the terms used in French cooking.

Now, put on your **un tablier** (apron) and enjoy!

Today, we will be learning all about emotional expression, speaking with eloquence, and becoming a French theatre and poetry expert.

"Talking Pretty" with French Liaison

La Prononciation: Pronunciation

What is it, you ask, that makes French sound so darn pretty? The not-so-secret secret for those in the know is *liaison*.

You know how we say *an owl* instead of *a owl* in English? Have you ever wondered why? It is because *a owl* produces awkward and choppy flow of pronunciation due to two vowels being placed next to each other. The simple answer is, it does not sound pretty. Somewhere in the evolution of the English language, the **n** was added to create flow between **a** and a word starting with a vowel. Liaison is kind of like that.

In French, liaison typically takes a traditionally silent consonant (like **deux**, or *two*) at the end of a word and changes it so that it is blended and linked up with the following word beginning with a vowel or mute **h** (like **amis**, or *friends*). The resulting pronunciation looks like this:

Example:

Deux **[deu]** + Amis **[ah mee]** = **[deu zah mee]**

Note: Many liaison forms tend to add a **z** or **t** sound to create the link between the two words. Keep this in mind as you note the various examples.

It may sound strange to foreigners, but just like its name, liaison links two words together to create quick, fluid speech. Turning **a** and *apple* into the pronunciation hybrid that sounds a lot like one word ("anapple") would sound strange to foreigners as well, so know that you are not alone.

Liaison is another one of those otherworldly exceptions that seems like a magical formula to the foreign ear. Trust me, there is a method to this madness, and once you have it mastered, your own muscle memory will automatically integrate it into your speech, just like we do in English. Saying it the improper way just will not "sound right" anymore.

There are two different types of liaison that we will be focusing on today.

They are **required** and **forbidden**.

Required Liaisons

Required liaisons are exactly what they sound like: required. They are universally pronounced, and this makes them the most important to remember.

1. Nominal Group

ARTICLE, NUMBER, or ADJECTIVE + NOUN or ADJECTIVE

Listen Track 34:

un **h**ome	[uh(n) nuhm]*
le**s a**mis	[lay za mee]
deu**x e**nfants	[deu za(n) fa(n)]
me**s é**lèves	[may zay lev]
peti**t a**mi	[peu tee ta mee]
le**s a**ncien**s é**lèves	[lay za(n) sye(n) zay lev]

2. Verbal Group

Pronoun + Verb or Adjective or Verb + Pronoun or Pronoun + Pronoun

Listen Track 35:

Vou**s a**vez	[vu za vay]
On**t-i**ls	[o(n) teel]
Nou**s en a**vons	[nu za(n) na vo(n)]

3. Single Syllable Adverbs, Conjunctions, and Prepositions

Listen Track 36:

tou**t e**ntier	[tu ta(n) tyay]
che**z e**lle	[shay zel]
trè**s u**tile	[tre zu teel]
bie**n é**trange	[bye nay tra(n)zh]
quan**d o**n décidera	[ka(n) to(n)]

4. Quand / est-ce que ***

Listen Track 37:

Quand est-ce que	[ka(n) te skeu]

5. Many Fixed Expressions – here are just a few examples:

Listen Track 38:

c'est-à-dire	[say ta deer]
avant hier	[a va(n) tyer]
plus ou moins	[plu zu mwa(n)]
comment allez-vous ?	[ko ma(n) ta lay vu]

Forbidden Liaisons

Forbidden liaisons could be referred to as an anti-liaison exception. In these instances, the liaison **must not** be pronounced. This exception arises when employing pronunciation would cause confusion (like using liaison on a name) or when using liaison would sound too much like another phrase.

Example:

Manon est parti. Manon left.

In this instance, liaison between **Manon**, a French girl's name, and **est** would not be useful. It would mar the purity of the pronunciation of **Manon** as a name. Along with this, **est parti** is the past tense conjugation of the verb **partir**, which means *to leave*. Because **est** is part of the past tense conjugation, utilizing liaison could also cause confusion as to whether we are really using the past tense.

Here are some specific instances where forbidden liaisons are used:

1. After a singular noun

Listen Track 39:

l'étudiant est prêt.   [lay tu dya(n) ay]

un garçon intelligent   [gar so(n) e(n) te lee zha(n)]

2. After names

Listen Track 40:

Thomas **e**st parti	[to ma ay par tee]
Alber**t a** une copine	[al ber a oon cuh peen]

3. After et (*and*)

Listen Track 41:

en haut **et e**n bas	[e(n) o ay a(n) ba]
un garçon **et u**ne fille	[u(n) gar so(n) ay un feey]

4. In front of an h aspiré

Listen Track 42:

les **h**éros	[lay ay ro]
en **h**aut	[a(n) o]

5. In front of onze and oui

Listen Track 43:

les **o**nze élèves	[lay o(n) zay lev]**
un **o**ui et un non	[u(n) wee ay u(n) no(n)]

6. After interrogative adverbs *** and toujours

Listen Track 44:

Combie**n e**n avez-vous ?	[ko(n) bye(n) a(n) na vay vu]
Commen**t e**st-il ?	[ko(n) ma(n) ay teel]
Quan**d a**s-tu mangé ?	[ka(n) a tu ma(n) zhay]
toujour**s i**ci	[tu zhu ree see]

7. After inversion

Listen Track 45:

Sont-il**s a**rrivés ?	[so(n) tee la ree vay]
Vont-elle**s a**ssister ?	[vo(n) teh la see stay]
A-t-o**n é**tudié ?	[a to(n) ay tu dyay]
Parlez-vou**s a**nglais	[par lay vu a(n) gleh]

In closing, liaison is something you will come across every single day of your journey through the French language. Learning it will make you sound more and more like a native speaker, and keeping it in mind when others are speaking will help you to recognize words affected by it and not be tripped up.

Le Vocabulaire: Vocabulary

Emotional Intelligence: French Emotions and Feelings

Now that we have a good amount of English and French cognates under our belt, it is time to learn some totally unfamiliar vocabulary. Today will be all about emotions and feelings. French movies, literature, art, and politics tend to make use of passionate expressions, so this vocabulary will serve you well in both expressing yourself and discussing the latest films.

Emotions

Listen Track 46:

le bonheur – happiness

la colère – anger

le contentement – contentment

l'ennui – boredom

l'envie – longing

la jalousie – jealousy

la satisfaction – satisfaction

la tristesse – sadness

la douleur – pain, grief

Positive feelings

Listen Track 47:

affectueux, affectueuse – affectionate

heureux, heureuse – happy

aux anges – on top of the world (literal translation: *with the angels*)

joyeux, joyeuse – joyful

ravi(e) – delighted, pleased

mieux – better

enthousiaste – excited

détendu(e) – relaxed

pensif, pensive – pensive

amusé(e) – amused

satisfait(e) – content

fier, fière – proud

nostalgique – nostalgic

amoureux, amoureuse – in love

inspiré, inspirée – inspired

de bonne humeur – in good spirits

fou de joie, folle de joie – elated

plein de vivacité(e) – high-spirited

étonné(e) – surprised

timide – bashful, shy

curieux, curieuse – curious

Negative feelings

Listen Track 48:

malheureux, malheureuse – unhappy

en colère, fâché(e) – angry

furieux, furieuse – furious

seul(e) – lonely

triste – sad

inquiet, inquiète – worried

ennuyé(e) – annoyed

jaloux, jalouse – jealous

désespéré(e) – desperate

déçu(e) – disappointed

occupé(e) – busy

préoccupé(e) – preoccupied

paresseux(euse) – lazy

mou, molle, apathique – apathetic

pressé(e) – in a hurry

absurde – silly, foolish

offensé(e) – offended

l'esprit de l'escalier – the feeling of thinking of a clever comeback after it is too late (literal translation: *staircase mind/wit*)

Discussing mental and physical lack of wellness

Listen Track 49:

anxieux(euse) – anxious

effrayé(e) – scared

déprimé(e) – depressed

fatigué(e) – tired

mauvais, mauvaise – not feeling well

cassé(e) – broken (denoting extreme exhaustion or malaise)

malade – sick

dégoûté(e) – disgusted

désorienté(e), perdu(e) – confused

paniqué(e) – panicky

maladroit(e) – clumsy

affamé(e) – hungry

assoiffé(e) – thirsty

La Grammaire: Grammar: To Be, or Not To Be? Être, the "To Be" Verb

The "to be" verb? No, this is not Shakespeare, but **être** is every bit the existential question it seems to be. Universally the first verb you learn in any language, "I am..." opens up the world of expression. This verb is so important that you are fated to be a conversation wallflower without it.

Since this is the first verb we are learning, there are a few things to know before we jump in. Just like in English, French uses infinitives as the base form of their verbs. **Être** is the infinitive of the verb *to be*.

When we conjugate each verb, French has a nifty formula for each pronoun. While these formulas differ somewhat, most follow a pattern. **Être** is an irregular verb, so its formula is unique to other verbs, which is not so bad given you will be using it all the time.

Remember each pronoun? Let's have a mini-recap:

Je – I	**Nous – we**
Te – you	**Vous – you (formal)**
Il/elle – he/she	**Ils/elles – they**

When we encounter French verb charts, they will follow this exact pattern, so each verb will have six conjugations.

Since we are just starting, we will stick with the utmost basics of the present, past, and future tenses. There will be further instruction in the days ahead, so view this as a friendly taste of what is to come. Memorizing the tenses for this verb is what we are really after today.

Être: Le Présent (Present Tense)

Listen Track 50:

Je suis	Nous sommes
Tu es	Vous êtes
Il/elle est	Ils/elles sont

Passé Composé: A Brief Overview of the Present Perfect Tense

The most common past tense form, the present perfect tense is used to:

- Denote an action completed in the past.

   Hier, j'ai vu mes sœurs.

   Yesterday, I saw my sisters.

Remember, this action must be completed. A good indicator of whether or not to use the passé composé is to ask yourself when it happened. If it was yesterday, today, Monday, last week, or last year (a specified time), then it is passé composé. If it was when you were little, every Saturday, or any other term indicating habitual activity, then you will use imparfait.

Être: Le Passé Composé (Present Perfect Tense)

Listen Track 51:

J'ai été	Nous avons été
Tu as été	Vous avez été
Il/elle a été	Ils/elles ont été

Imparfait: A Brief Overview of the Imperfect Tense

For our current objectives, the imperfect tense is used to:

- Indicate habitual actions in the past.

   Quand J'étais petite, j'allais au cinéma avec ma famille.

   When I was little, I would go to the movie theater with my family.

- Express time, weather, age, and feelings.

   J'étais heureux qu'il faisait beau.

   I was happy that the weather was nice.

Être: Imparfait (Imperfect Tense)

Listen Track 52:

J'étais	Nous étions
Tu étais	Vous étiez
Il/elle était	Ils/elles étaient

Le Futur: A Brief Overview of the Future Tense

Fairly straightforward, the future tense in French indicates:

- An action that will happen in the future.

  Je serai triste de partir.

I will be sad to leave.

- If/then statements.

  Si j'ai le temps, je mangerai quelque chose.

If I have the time, I will eat something.

Etre: Le Futur (Future Tense)

Listen Track 53:

Je serai	**Nous serons**
Tu seras	**Vous serez**
Il/elle sera	**Ils/elles seront**

Note: We just learned liaison, and this verb puts it to good use. Remember that "**Je suis américain**" will be pronounced just like "Je suis-**zah**-méricain."

La Conversation: Speaking

Once More, with Feeling: Using Emotional Expressions

Since we just learned our French emotions, now we will learn how to use them in a sentence. Discussing emotions in French is incredibly satisfying. French is a language of love, after all, so you know it has emotional expressions in abundance.

It is worth noting that there are quite a few different ways to say "I feel..." in French. Some emotions carry exceptional forms, so keep an eye out for those and memorize them.

Whether you are flirting along the Seine or channeling your inner beatnik at a Parisian café (or, you know, just normally expressing yourself), these emotional expressions are the golden ticket to eloquence.

Ways to Express Emotion:

1. **Se sentir, the "to feel" verb**

2. **a/ Sentir: to feel**

Listen Track 54:

Je me sens	Nous nous sentons
Tu te sens	Vous vous sentez
Il/elle se sent	Ils/elles se sentent

Examples:

Listen Track 55:

Je me sens heureux/heureuse. – I feel happy.

Je me sens joyeux/joyeuse. – I feel content.

Je me sens timide. – I feel shy.

Je me sens vivant(e). – I feel alive.

b/ Je suis... – I am

Examples:

Listen Track 56:

Je suis triste. – I'm sad.

Je suis content(e). – I'm content.

Je suis fatigué(e). – I'm tired.

Specific Exceptions for Expressions:

Listen Track 57:

Je t'aime. – I love you.

Je m'ennuie. – I'm bored.

J'ai peur. – I'm scared.

J'ai soif. – I'm thirsty.

J'ai faim. – I'm hungry.

French Colloquial Phrases:

Listen Track 58:

Je suis en pleine forme. – I'm in good shape.

Je suis de tout cœur avec toi. – I feel deeply for you.

Je suis sur un petit nuage! – I'm on cloud nine!

Je suis de bonne humeur. – I'm in a good mood.

Je m'en fiche. – I could care less.

Occupe-toi de tes oignons! – Mind your own business!

Je meurs d'ennui. – I'm dying of boredom.

C'est ma bête noire. – It's my pet peeve.

J'en ai jusque-là. – I've had it up to here.

Oh là là! – Oh my!

Ah bon? – Oh really?

C'est n'est pas ma tasse de thé. – It's not my cup of tea.

Bien fait pour toi! – Serves you right!

La vache! – Holy cow!

Après nous, le déluge. – I don't care.

Quel dommage! – What a shame!

C'est penible! – What a pain!

L'Immersion: Immersion

Of Art and Pirate Hearts: French Pop, Poetry, and Plays

Film du jour: Film of the Day

"Phèdre" – Racine

We are taking a bit of a detour today. Since we learned all about French emotional expression, why not channel our inner diva (or divo) and go to the (virtual) theatre today?

Along with Molière and Corneille, Jean Racine (1639-1699) is France's answer to Shakespeare. His tragedies are numerous and full of pathos, and his tendency toward adapting famous Greek works further solidified his claim to fame as a tragedian and dramatist. Finding steady work throughout the 17th century, he was made a member of l'académie française, worked closely with the king as treasurer and secretary, and even put on plays for the king's children at the queen's behest. All that to say, he was, and still is, a pretty big deal. In terms of style, Racine was very minimalist for his time. He favored writing plays with few characters and very little action beyond dialog. As was in fashion at the time, he wrote in rhyming "alexandrine" verse, which boasted lines of twelve syllables. His use of this style allowed his polished, elegant dialog to shine. His plays focus on the misfortune of royalty intimately and unreservedly. Since his plays oftentimes pull from Greek tragedy, there is an overarching theme of lack of control over one's destiny and inability to reverse prophecy. Romance is almost always obsessional in his plays, making for some decidedly over-the-top drama. Some of his most famous plays are *Andromaque* (1667), *Britannicus* (1669), *Iphigénie* (1674), and *Phèdre*, but we will be focusing on *Phèdre* today. While her husband (Thésée, the King of Athens) is away, Phèdre expresses her forbidden love for Hippolyte, his son from another marriage. What ensues is juicy, juicy drama. Try to find Patrice Chereau's adaptation of the famous play. The set design and costumes are startlingly modern in contrast with the style of speech. Dominique Blanc as "Phèdre" is a force to be reckoned with.

Musique du jour: Music of the Day

Cœur du Pirate

Coeur du Pirate (translated as "Pirate's Heart") is a Canadian songstress of high merit. Rising to fame for her sweet voice, thoughtful lyrics, and eclectic persona, she currently has the French music scene in the palm of her hand.

Also known as a competent composer and pianist, there is a lot to love about Coeur du Pirate. Her self-titled debut album is simple and piano-driven, while her sophomore offering, *Blonde*, has a grander scale with a '60s vibe. "Comme des Enfants," "Adieu," and "Place de la République" are all great places to start.

Oh, and her latest album is in English, so you can feel free to enjoy her in two languages. You're welcome.

L'activite du jour: Activity of the Day

Poetry is highly revered in France. Just like English, there are a multitude of movements and styles that make up the French poetical canon. Today, we are going to focus on a famous poem by a modern poet.

Jacques Prévert (1900-1977) was part of the French realist and surrealist movements. This means that he shunned traditional rhyming schemes and structure for simplicity and subtle impact. The poetic realist movement of the 1930s favored a nihilistic, dismal view on life, and much of Prévert's poetry leans toward this. Even so, he also weaves together heartrendingly tender odes to admiring the small joys of life and the beauty of innocence. Here he is, in full form, with "Dejeuner du Matin." There is an English translation below, but try to use your French dictionary first to piece out what he is saying. Hint: There is a lot of passé compose.

"Déjeuner du matin"

-Jacques Prévert

Listen Track 59:

Il a mis le café

Dans la tasse

Il a mis le lait Dans la tasse de café

Il a mis le sucre

Dans le café au lait

Avec la petite cuiller

Il a tourné

Il a bu le café au lait

Et il a reposé la tasse

Sans me parler

Il a allumé

Une cigarette

Il a fait des ronds

Avec la fumée

Il a mis les cendres

Dans le cendrier

Sans me parler

Sans me regarder

Il s'est levé

Il a mis

Son chapeau sur sa tête

Il a mis son manteau de pluie

Parce qu'il pleuvait

Et il est parti

Sous la pluie

Sans une parole

Sans me regarder

Et moi j'ai pris

Ma tête dans ma main

Et j'ai pleuré

"Breakfast"

-Jacques Prévert

He poured the coffee

Into the cup

He put the milk

Into the cup of coffee

He put the sugar

Into the coffee with milk

With a small spoon

He churned

He drank the coffee

And he put down the cup

Without any word to me

He lit

One cigarette

He made circles

With the smoke

He shook off the ash

Into the ashtray

Without any word to me

Without any look at me

He got up

He put on

His hat on his head

He put on

His raincoat

Because it was raining

And he left

Into the rain

Without any word to me

Without any look at me

And I buried

My face in my hands

And I cried.

Pretty deep, huh? There is also a prize-winning short film depicting this poem directed by Emmanuel Tenenbaum that is worth checking out as well. Jacques Prévert's poetry is great for learning, as his simplistic structure makes it easy to pick out patterns. Feel free to check out more!

Chapter 4 – Day 4
Bon Appétit! French Gastronomy

Today, we will touch on French cuisine vocabulary, ordering at restaurants in French, and how to negate sentences.

La Prononciation: Pronunciation

The Throaty French "R"

The good old French "R" sound is part of what makes French sound French. It is also one of the more difficult pronunciations for English-speakers, but have no fear! There are some tried and true tricks that will have you belting it out with the best of them.

What makes the French "R" so difficult is that it really does not sound or feel like the English "R," much less any other sound in the English language. Instead of being pronounced in front of your mouth, the French "R" is formed by elevating the back of the tongue and essentially trilling against the uvula (that fleshy extension of the soft palate that hangs down above your throat).

This is called an uvular fricative. By barely touching the tongue against the uvula, friction can take place as air passes through. What ensues is a raspy, guttural sound that kind of feels like you are channeling your inner cat and coughing up a hairball.

The closest thing we have to this in English is the "Z" sound. Even though it is pronounced in the front of the mouth, we still get that vibration from the friction created by air passing through the tip of the tongue and roof of the mouth.

So, let's try it. The best way to start is by relaxing your mouth.

Step 1: Place your fist under your jaw (like you are back in elementary school and posing for an awkward yearbook photo).

Step 2: Using your fist as resistance, open your mouth slightly and push your jaw against the fist.

Step 3: Count to eight in your head.

Step 4: Relax your jaw for three seconds.

Repeat this two or three times, or until your jaw and mouth feel relaxed. If your tongue feels tense, stick it out and stretch it a couple of times until it feels relaxed as well.

Now we can focus on getting the feel of pronouncing this sound:

Step 1: Open your mouth.

Step 2: Close your throat as if you are going to gargle or to avoid swallowing a mouthful of liquid, and say **K** carefully, several times.

Step 3: Pay attention to where in your throat the **K** sound is made. We will call this the *K place.*

Step 4: Begin slowly closing your throat, until you can almost feel the **K** place. Your throat should be only partially constricted.

Step 5: Tense the muscles around the K place.

Step 6: Gently push air through your partially constricted throat.

Step 7: Practice saying Ra-Ra-Ra (where R = steps 4-6) every day.

Another method for practicing this involves slowly tricking your mouth into forming the sound:

Step 1: Say "A-AB" multiple times.

Step 2: Now say "A-HAB" multiple times.

Step 3: Once you feel ready, try to say "A-HRAB". It should sound like a throaty version of the word "Arab".

Step 4: Continue with "A-HRAB" until you notice a distinct "R" sound forming.

Step 5: Attempt to isolate this sound and try it with French "R" words.

And that's that. Once you have mastered this sound, you will also notice that many French-speakers tend to breeze through it as they speak, softening the friction by barely touching the back of their tongue against the uvula. This will come naturally along with practice and further development in the language, so do not be self-conscious if your "R" is a little throatier than the others.

Note: Some compare this sound to the trill of the Spanish "R" and emulate that so as to improve their French "R," but you might get some funny stares if you embrace that. The two sounds are pronounced in completely different parts of the mouth, so leave the rolling "R" to the Spanish-speakers.

Le Vocabulaire: Vocabulary

Apples and Oranges: French Food Vocabulary

The quality of cuisine in France is world-renowned, and the country takes steps every day to keep it that way. Because of this, French grocery stores and restaurants tend to carry more locally-grown and non-GMO foods, meaning much of what you are buying and eating is fresher.

When you are working with fresh fish, dairy, and produce, it changes the way you shop and cook. It allows for seasonal recipes to be enjoyed based on produce availability throughout the year. Farmer's markets and local food experts are valued, so artisanal cheeses and specialty items are plentiful, even in supermarkets. Independent bakeries and butchers are literally everywhere. And yogurt, made with fresh dairy, has its very own aisle.

Suffice it to say that shopping, cooking, and eating in France is a totally different experience. Due to this fresher approach to cuisine, the French shopping method generally dictates that one should allot time each day for going to the grocery store and buying just enough groceries to prepare meals for that day. Because of this, many people (especially in the city) will walk to the store, buy the small amount they need, and carry their miniature bounty back home.

Knowing this is important when it comes to learning the vocabulary. Since much of your food experiences in France will be completely different from what you are used to, vocabulary is the anchor you can rely on when navigating this new terrain. Especially when you are ordering food at a restaurant, this vocabulary will help you pick out the key words for all those fancy French dishes you have always wanted to try.

French Food:

Listen Track 60:

la nourriture – food

le repas – meal

le petit-déjeuner – breakfast

le déjeuner – lunch

le diner – dinner

le hors d'œuvre – appetizer

l'entrée – a starter

le goûter – snack

le plat principal – main course

la soupe, le potage – soup

la salade – salad

le dessert – dessert

manger (verb) – to eat

déjeuner (verb) – to have breakfast or lunch

diner (verb) – to have dinner

la cuisine – kitchen, cooking

la salle à manger – dining room

le restaurant – restaurant

French Fruits:

Listen Track 61:

le fruit – fruit

un abricot – apricot

un ananas – pineapple

une banane – banana

une cerise – cherry

un citron – lemon

un citron vert – lime

une fraise – strawberry

une framboise – raspberry

une mûre – blackberry

une myrtille – blueberry

une orange – orange

un pamplemousse – grapefruit

une **pastèque** – watermelon

une **pêche** – peach

une **poire** – pear

une **pomme** – apple

une **prune** – plum

un **raisin** – grape

French Vegetables:

Listen Track 62:

un **légume** – vegetable

un **artichaut** – artichoke

les **asperges (f)** – asparagus

une **aubergine** – eggplant

la **carotte** – carrot

le **céleri** – celery

le **champignon** – mushroom

le **chou-fleur** – cauliflower

le **concombre** – cucumber

les **épinards (m)** – spinach

la **laitue** – lettuce

un **oignon** – onion

le **maïs** – corn

les **petits pois (m)** – peas

la **pomme de terre** – potato

le **radis** – radish

la **tomate** – tomato

Meat:

Listen Track 63:

la **viande** – meat

l'agneau (m) – lamb

les anchois (m) – anchovies

le bifteck – steak

la dinde – turkey

les escargots (m) – snails

le jambon – ham

le lapin – rabbit

le poisson – fish

le porc – pork

le poulet – chicken

le rosbif – roast beef

le saucisson – sausage

le veau – veal

Dairy:

Listen Track 64:

le beurre – butter

la crème – cream

la crème fraîche – very thick, slightly sour cream

le fromage – cheese

le fromage blanc – cream cheese

la glace – ice cream

le lait – milk

le yaourt – yogurt

Dessert:

Listen Track 65:

le dessert – dessert

le biscuit – cookie

les bonbons – candy

le chocolat – chocolate

la crème caramel – flan

les fruits (m) – fruit

le gâteau – cake

la glace – ice cream

la mousse au chocolat – chocolate mousse

la tarte – pie

la vanille – vanilla

French Staples:

Listen Track 66:

la confiture – jam

le croissant – croissant

la farine – flour

les frites – (US) fries, (UK) chips

l'huile d'olive (f) – olive oil

la mayonnaise – mayonnaise

la moutarde – mustard

un œuf, des œufs – egg, eggs

le pain – bread

le pain grillé – toast

les pâtes – pasta

le poivre – pepper

le riz – rice

la sauce – sauce, dressing, gravy

le sel – salt

le sucre – sugar

Drinks:

Listen Track 67:

un apéritif – pre-dinner drink, cocktail

le café – coffee

la bière – beer

le champagne – champagne

le digestif – after-dinner drink

l'eau – water

l'eau minéral – mineral water

le jus d'orange – orange juice

le jus de pomme – apple juice

le lait – milk

le soda – soda

le thé – tea

une bouteille de vin – a bottle of wine

le vin rouge – red wine

le vin blanc – white wine

La Grammaire – Grammar: The Art of Saying No: French Negation

La négation, or French negation, is fairly simple. There are a few exceptions to consider, though, so today we will focus on mastering the basics and moving on to exceptions.

The most basic (and most common) way to negate a sentence in French is to place **ne** before a verb and **pas** after, as in:

Example:

Je ne suis pas fatigué. I am not tired.

Suis is the **je** form of **être** (to be), so utilizing the **ne…pas** form puts a negative spin on the sentence.

Let's try another, this time using a verb starting with a vowel.

Example:

Non, elle n'aime pas la musique classique. No, she does not like classical music.

In this instance, we used the verb **aimer** (to like, love). When the verb begins with a vowel, we drop the **e** and replace it with an apostrophe. Otherwise, the fluidity of pronunciation would be compromised.

Let's try one more, this time using **ne…jamais** (never):

Example:

Je ne chante jamais. I never sing.

By utilizing the **ne…jamais** form with the verb **chanter** (to sing), we are able to intensify the negation from "I don't sing" to "I never sing."

The **ne…pas** form sandwiches between the verb it is negating for **imparfait** and **le futur**, but it is a little different when it comes to **passé composé**.

Negating Passé Composé:

We touched on the present perfect tense briefly when we went over conjugated forms of **être**. We're going to build upon that foundation by negating **être** in passé composé, both as an auxiliary verb and a past participle. To do that, though, we are going to need to break down this tense even further.

You may have noticed that passé composé is a compound verb tense, meaning that it possesses two parts. The first is the present tense of the auxiliary verb, which will always be either **être** (to be) or **avoir** (to have), depending on the past participle of the verb we are working with. This past participle is the second part of the passé composé. So, the formula for this tense is:

CONJUGATED AUXILIARY VERB + PAST PARTICIPLE

Example:

Je suis allé au cinéma hier. I went to the movie theater yesterday.

This sentence used passé composé on **aller** (to go). As you can see, we conjugated the auxiliary verb **être** in the present tense. The past participle of **aller** is **allé**, so we place this directly after the auxiliary verb.

Now, let's try one with **être**, which uses **avoir** as the auxiliary verb.

Example:

Elle a été malade toute la nuit. She was sick all night.

We conjugated **avoir** in the present tense to form our auxiliary verb; **été** is the past participle of **être**, so this is placed after the auxiliary verb.

Now that we understand the breakdown of passé composé, we can implement negation with this formula in mind. Since passé composé is compound, **ne...pas** takes on a bit of a different twist. In this tense, the **ne...pas** is sandwiched around the conjugated auxiliary verb.

Example:

Je ne suis pas allé au cinéma. I didn't go to the movies.

The only exceptions to this are **ne...nulle part** (nowhere), **ne...personne** (anyone), and **ne...aucun(e)** (any). These are always placed around the whole compound verb.

Example:

Je ne suis allé nulle part. I didn't go anywhere.

Example:

Il n'a vu personne. He didn't see anyone.

Example:

Je n'ai eu aucun respect pour lui. I didn't have any respect for him.

Note: Aucun depends on the noun following it, so if the noun is feminine, change it to **aucune**.

La Conversation - Speaking: More Escargot, Please / Ordering Food at a Restaurant

You know your food vocabulary, so it is time to put that to good use. Here are some sentences you should know before digging in.

Arriving:

Listen Track 68:

J'ai reservé une table au nom de... – I reserved a table under the name…

Avez-vous une table pour deux? – Do you have a table for two?

Je voudrais une table près de la fenêtre. – I would like a table near the window.

Je voudrais un box, s'il vous plait – I would like a booth, please.

Ordering:

Listen Track 69:

Vous avez choisi? – Have you decided?

Que voudriez-vous? – What would you like?

Est-ce que vous voulez quelque chose à boire pour commencer ? – Would you like something to drink to start with?

Que prenez-vous? – What are you having?

Je suis prêt(e) à commander – I'm ready to order

Un moment, s'il vous plaît. – One moment, please.

Je ne sais pas encore. – I don't know yet.

Je voudrais… – I would like… (polite)

J'aimerais… – I would like…

Je vais prendre/Je prends – I'll have…

Preferences:

Listen Track 70:

Je suis – I am...

végétarien/végétarienne – vegetarian

végétalien/végétalienne – vegan

bleu, saignant – bloody rare

rosé – rare

à point – medium-well

bien cuit – well done

All about the menu:

Listen Track 71:

Quel est le plat du jour? – What is today's special?

Est-ce que vous avez des recommandations/une spécialité/une suggestion? – Do you have any recommendations/specialties/suggestions?

Quelle sorte de légumes avez-vous? – What sort of vegetables do you have?

Je voudrais la carte des vins, s'il vous plait. – I would like the wine menu, please.

Est-ce que c'est possible d'avoir... – Is it possible to have...

un morceau – a piece

une tranche – a slice (of meat, cake, bread)

une rondelle – a slice (fruit, veggie)

à la carte – A style of dining where the diner selects individual dishes.

prix fixe – A French dining style where they group several courses into one fixed price.

à la vapeur – steamed

à l'etouffée – stewed

au four – baked

bouilli – boiled

en daube – in a stew

fondu – melted

fumé – smoked

grillé – grilled

haché – minced (ground)

frit – fried

Allergies:

Listen Track 72:

Je suis allergique à… – I'm allergic to…

aux noix – to nuts

aux cacahuètes – to peanuts

aux fruits de mer – to shellfish

aux produits laitiers – to dairy products

au soja – to soy

au blé – to wheat

au gluten – to gluten

aux œufs – to eggs

Asking for the Check:

Listen Track 73:

L'addition, s'il vous plait. – Check, please.

C'est terminé – We're finished eating.

Nous sommes ensemble. – We're together (on the check).

Nous paierons séparément. – We'll pay separately.

Je vais payer avec ma carte de crédit. – I'm going to pay with my credit card.

Je crois qu'il y a une erreur dans l'addition. – I believe there's an error on the bill.

Vous étiez un serveur merveilleux. – You were an excellent server.

Acceptez-vous les pourboires? – Do you accept tips?

Service compris – tip included

Service non compris – tip not included

L'Immersion: Immersion - On Va au Resto! French Restaurants and Electropop

Le Film du Jour: Film of the Day

"Haute Cuisine (Les Sauveurs du Palais)"

Haute Cuisine, released as *Les Saveurs du Palais* in France, is the perfect choice for today's theme. The biopic focuses on the trials and triumphs of Danièle Delpeuch, a small-town chef of great renown who is appointed as the private chef of President Francois Mitterand. The film is a smorgasbord of mouth-watering haute cuisine dishes, but it also touches on gender politics specific to France. Delpeuch, immediately singled out in an all-male workplace, pushes past the jealousy and sexism to establish herself as a culinary icon. Since this film is all about cooking and serving, keep your ears open for what we have already learned along with other vocab morsels.

La musique du jour: Music of the Day

Yelle

After all that food, some danceable pop is in high order. Yelle is more than happy to oblige. Created by Yelle (Julie Budet) and GrandMarnier (Jean-Francois Perrier) in 2000, the band exploded onto the French music charts after "Je Veux Te Voir," a song railing against French rapper Cuisiner of TTC, went viral on Myspace. Yelle herself is the poster child for French electropop. While her voice and beats are sugary sweet, it is her sharp tongue and quirky, irreverent spirit that keeps us coming back for more. The band's lyrics are also very much on the up and up of French slang and everyday speech, so you will be getting a lesson on how to adopt an effortlessly cool speaking style. Yelle currently has three albums to their name. *Pop-Up* leans more on the pop side of things, and *Safari Disco Club* and *Complètement Fou* progress toward a heavier electronic influence.

L'Activité du Jour: Activity of the Day

Aller au Restaurant français: Go to a French Restaurant

The best cumulative practice of all that we have learned this week is to go straight to the source. So, **on va au resto!** That's slang for, "Let's go to a restaurant!" If you can, find an authentic French restaurant near you and make a reservation. Once you are there, tell the server that you want to practice speaking French. **"Puis-je pratiquer mon français, s'il vous plait?"** (May I practice my French, please?) will do the trick. You can bring along a cheat sheet and add notes on other words and phrases you pick up.

If you do not happen to have any French restaurants in your area, hit up a French bakery or cultural club in your area. Many cultural clubs host food events where you can practice the language with native speakers and other learners, so you definitely will not be missing out. It is worth noting that dining in France is an event in itself. Meals consisting of several courses are savored, sometimes over several hours, and conversation is in abundance. It is not uncommon for diners to follow the meal with dessert or coffee (or dessert, then coffee). This allows for more time to enjoy the atmosphere and company.

That is why getting these phrases down will benefit you so much in the long-run. Restaurants and cafés are sacred places where the purpose is not just to eat and leave. It is an experience characterized by two or more hours of talking, both with the waiter and whoever comes with you, so getting the basics down is the key to relishing the experience.

Bon appétit et à demain! (Have a good meal and see you tomorrow!)

Chapter 5 – Day 5
Finding Direction

Today, we will touch on the French "U," asking for and understanding directions, and the role of race, religion, and gender in France.

La Prononciation: Pronunciation - The Elusive French "U"

Now that your French "R" is getting a good workout, it is time to introduce our next contender: the French "U."

This sound eludes many learners simply because it does not exist in the English language. The closest comparison would be the "OU" sound, as in *you*, but even that is not quite right. French has that "OU" sound, too, and the sound we are after is created closer to the front of the mouth. In order to fight against our natural inclination to associate the French "U" with the "OU" we are familiar with, we will be directing part of this lesson toward making the distinction in French.

The French "U" is a close front-rounded vowel, which means it is:

- pronounced with the tip of your tongue close to the roof of your mouth (close)
- situated at the front of your mouth (front)
- made by making an "O" with your lips (rounded)

Now we can work toward pronouncing this sound:

Step 1: Open your mouth.

Step 2: Say "O".

Step 3: Draw out the "O" until your lips are where they would be to make a "W" sound.

Step 4: Purse your lips as tightly as you can.

Step 5: Keeping your lips pursed, say "E".

Step 6: Voilà! The French "U"

Another method for practicing uses the French "E," a close front *unrounded* vowel, as a tool to get us to the close front-*rounded* "U."

Step 1: Make the French "E" sound (as in **fini**). English has the same sound, so it should sound something like the "E" sound in *me* or *glee*.

Step 2: Once you have this sound, hold it out. Notice that your lips are pulled taut toward your cheeks as though you are smiling. This is the unrounded part of the vowel.

Step 3: While still making the "E" sound, slowly move your lips into a rounded "O." Note the change in sound. It should now sound exactly like the French "U."

Step 4: You did it! Keep practicing this, exaggerating both sound and facial movements.

Did you notice that the French "U" has a very different feel and sound from the "OU" we are familiar with? Even so, it is still much more difficult to notice this distinction when your mind is busy with the multi-tasking that comes along with conversing in a foreign language. Let us take a closer look at these differences.

Differentiating Between "U" and "OU"

The best way to understand just how distinct these two sounds are is to compare similar words. This helps you note the differences in pronunciation while recognizing that a lot of these words have very different meanings. Learning the difference will help you avoid needless confusion.

Note: Remember that the French "OU" is very similar to the English "OU" sound, as in *group*.

Listen Track 74:

la hutte (hut)

août (August)

nu (nude)

nous (we)

la bulle (bubble)

la boule (ball)

la rue (street)

la roue (wheel)

su (knew)

sous (under)

la mule (mule)

la moule (mussel)

lu (read)

le loup (wolf)

vu (saw)

vous (you, formal)

dessus (above)

dessous (below)

bu (drank)

la boue (mud)

tu (you, informal)

tout (all)

la puce (flea)

le pouce (thumb)

pur (pure)

pour (for)

sur (on)

sourd (deaf)

le jus (juice)

la joue (cheek)

rugi (roared)

rougi (blushed)

Le Vocabulaire- Vocabulary: Mapping Out a City in Words: French Place Names and Directional Vocab

Knowing how to say "restroom" and "water fountain" in another language is pretty much a survival skill. Knowing other words like "bakery" and "the historic district," though? Well, that can start to make the world around you a bit bigger, one place name at a time. In a foreign country, place names and directional vocabulary expand horizons, which is something every traveler seeks.

And that is the goal of today's lesson. We will be learning how to ask for directions later on today, but having these place names down is crucial. If you ever forget how to ask for something or are in an emergency situation and cannot think on your feet, knowing one simple word can make all the difference.

French Place Names:

Listen Track 75:

l'agence de voyage – travel agency

la banque – bank

le bar – bar

la boulangerie – bakery

le bureau de change – money exchange

le café – café

le centre historique – historic district

le centre-ville – town square, town center

le cinéma – movie theater

la discothèque, la boite (casual) – dance club

le distributeur automatique, le distributeur – ATM

l'église (f.) – church

l'épicerie (f.) – grocery store

la fontaine d'eau – water fountain

l'hôpital (m.) – hospital

'hôtel – hotel

la mairie – town hall

le musée – museum

le parc – park

la pizzeria – pizzeria

le pont – bridge

la poste – post office

le poste de police – police station

le Quartier Latin – the Latin Quarter (in Paris)

la rue – street

la rue commerciale – shopping district

le supermarché – supermarket

le théâtre – theater (for plays)

les toilettes, les WC – restroom

la tour Eiffel – the Eiffel Tower

Transportation:

Listen Track 76:

l'aéroport – airport

le bateau – boat

le bateau-mouche – tour boat

le bus – bus

le bus touristique – tour bus

le métro – subway, metro station

la station – metro station

la gare – train station

le TGV (train à grande vitesse) – high-speed train

le taxi – taxi

le train – train

la gare routière – bus station

la zone piétonne – pedestrian area

le passage piéton – pedestrian crossing

le sentier pédestre – pedestrian walkway

la piste cyclable – bike trail (off-road)

une moto – motorcycle

un vélo – bike

la voiture – car

la voiture de location – rental car

Directional Vocab:

Listen Track 77:

droite – right

gauche – left

le nord – north

le sud – south

l'est – east

l'ouest – west

La Grammaire- Grammar: Oh, There It Is: "Il y a"

Il y a, or *there is/are* is one of the most important grammar constructions to learn in French. It is made up of three parts:

il – it

y – there

a – conjugated form of **avoir** (to have)

There are three constructions you will encounter the most. They are:

1. **Il y a + INDEFINITE ARTICLE + NOUN**

<u>**Example**</u>:

Il y a un lapin dans la forêt. There's a rabbit in the forest.

2. **Il y a + NUMBER + NOUN**

<u>**Example**</u>:

Il y a deux oiseaux dans le jardin. There are two birds in the garden.

3. **Il y a + INDEFINITE PRONOUN**

<u>**Example**</u>:

Il y a quelqu'un à votre bureau. There is someone at your office.

You will occasionally see **il y a** paired with a period of time, which changes its meaning to *ago*.

<u>**Example**</u>:

Il y a trois semaines que je suis tombée amoureuse de lui.

I fell in love with him three weeks ago.

Conjugating "Il y a" for Imparfait and Le Futur:

Because the **a** in **il y a** is the third person singular conjugation of **avoir**, it is as simple as conjugating for the tense to say things like *there was* or *there will be*.

Let's take a look at the imparfait form first.

Example:

Il y avait un homme dans le tableau. There was a man in the painting.

The conjugation **a** is the third person singular form of **avoir**, which relates to he, she, and it. This means that we use **avait**, which is the third person singular imparfait form, for this sentence. Since we always use the third person singular **a** for the present tense of **il y a**, **avait** will always be used for imparfait. This makes it easy to remember.

Now we will see an example of **il y a** with le futur.

Example:

Il y aura des crocodiles dans le marais. There will be crocodiles in the swamp.

Since the third person singular future tense form of **avoir** is **aura**, we will always use this conjugation for the future tense of **il y a**.

Now we will use **il y a** to ask questions.

Asking Questions with "il y a":

There are two different ways to pose questions with **il y a**.

1. **Est-ce qu' + il y a**

Example:

Est-ce qu'il y a une réunion aujourd'hui? Is there a meeting today?

Est-ce que is an interrogative form that we will be seeing a lot of tomorrow. When it is paired with **il y a**, we must use an apostrophe after the **u** so the vowels **e** and **i** do not impede ease of pronunciation.

2. **Y a-t-il, or Inversion**

Inversion is where the normal order of French sentence structure (noun or pronoun + verb) is inverted to become verb + noun or pronoun. We will be discussing this more tomorrow, but it is important to memorize this interrogative form of **il y a**, as it is used often in everyday speech.

Example:

Y a-t-il un problème? Is there a problem?

With the inversion of **il y a**, we take the pronoun **y** and place it at the beginning, then flip the verb **a** and the pronoun **il**. Since **a** and **il** both start with a vowel, French often uses -**t**- to create liaison between the vowels.

Note: Y a-t-il is the only correct way to structure this phrase. You may see **y-a-t-il**, **y-a-t'il**, **y a t'il**, or other variations, but these are incorrect and should be avoided.

Negating with "Il y a":

To say *there isn't* or *there aren't*, you must add **n** before **y** and **pas** after the, along with **de** before any noun that comes after. This creates the following formula: **IL N'Y A PAS + DE + NOUN**

Example:

Il n'y a pas de solution. There isn't a solution.

Example:

Il n'y a pas de stylos. There are no pens.

All in all, the most important thing to remember with **il y a** and its variations is that your mastery of them is based on memorization. It may seem like there are a lot of pieces and parts to each formula, but these pieces and parts always stay the same. It is always conjugated in the third person singular of **avoir**, and both the interrogative and negation forms follow the same rules every time. This is another grammar point that comes up often in French, so using these phrases over and over will make them second nature.

La Conversation – Speaking: Where Am I? Asking for and Understanding Directions in French

With all of those place names you now have under your belt, asking for directions will be a piece of cake. The real challenge is understanding the directions given to you, so a large portion of these phrases will be used from the perspective of the person relaying information to you. I have underlined place names to indicate that it can be replaced with the place name of your choosing.

Asking:

Listen Track 78:

Où se trouve... – Where do I find…

Où est... – Where is…

Excusez-moi, est-ce que vous pouvez me dire où est <u>la bibliothèque</u>, s'il vous plait? – Excuse me, can you tell me where the library is, please? (formal)

Excuse-moi, est-ce que tu peux me dire où est <u>la tour Eiffel</u>, s'il te plait? – Excuse me, can you tell me where the Eiffel Tower is, please? (casual)

Est-ce que vous savez comment aller au<u> théâtre</u>? – Do you know how to get to the theater? (formal)

Est-ce que tu sais comment aller à <u>la boite</u>? – Do you know how to get to the club? (casual)

Ou est-ce que je peux trouver <u>le métro</u>, s'il vous plait? – Where can I find the metro, please?

Comment est-ce que je fais pour aller <u>au parc</u>? – How can I make my way to the park?

Understanding Directions:

Listen Track 79:

C'est/Il est – It's…

tourner – to turn

prendre – to take

aller – to go

marcher – to walk

suivre – follow

et puis – and then…

jusqu'à – until

arriver à destination – to arrive at your destination

à gauche – to the left

à droite – to the right

tout droit – straight

le coin – the corner

en face de – in front of

à l'arrière – behind

à côté de – next to

près de – near to

loin de – far from

au bout de – at the end of

au début de – at the beginning of

au coin de la rue – around the corner

au nord – to the north

au sud – to the south

à l'est – to the east

à l'ouest – to the west

la rue suivante – the next street

le panneau stop – stop sign

le feu de signalisation – traffic light

Tournez à droite, marchez tout droit jusqu'à la rue suivante, et puis arrêtez au feu de signalisation. – Turn right, walk straight until the next street, and then stop at the traffic light.

C'est au nord. Prends le métro jusqu'à <u>la gare du nord</u>, tourne à gauche et suis le chemin. – It's to the north. Take the train until the North Station, turn left and follow the pathway.

L'Immersion – Immersion: Taboo Talk, Gender, Race, and Religion Ethics in France

Le Film du Jour: Film of the Day

"Intouchables"

Intouchables (The Untouchables) has gotten a lot of attention since its 2011 release. Based on a true story, it is about a wealthy quadriplegic who hires an ex-con from the inner-city to be his caretaker. What ensues is a friendship that shatters the economic and social boundaries around them.

Touching and funny, this movie is more than meets the eye. It is a stellar example of the feel-good movie genre, but it also stands as a great commentary on race and religion ethics in France. From a language-learning perspective, you will be getting a lot of great conversation-ready vocabulary from the slow-moving dialogue and plot.

La Musique du Jour : Music of the Day

Stromae

The start of Stromae's career is a modern fairytale. It begins with a track called "Alors on Danse" and a bevy of YouTube videos on composing. Cut to 2009 and you have a national sensation. "Alors on Dance" reached the top of the music charts in twelve countries, propelling Stromae into the spotlight as Europe's next big thing. Former French president Nicolas Sarcozy admitted that he was crazy about his music. The Belgian Prime Minister gave President Obama Stromae's first album as a gift representative of Belgian culture. It truly goes without saying that the Belgian-Rwandan singer has become a huge household name. His discography is eclectic and multi-faceted, as he pulls from African, French folk, rap, hip hop, and electronic genres at will. "Papaoutai", another huge hit of his, pairs afro-pop with danceable electronic beats. "Tous Les Mêmes", a song detailing relational drama from both sides, got a lot of buzz with a music video where he split his persona in half between male and female as he sang from both perspectives. Whether it be cancer, a drunk man separated from his girlfriend, absentee fathers, or the carnivorous nature of social media, Stromae wants to talk about it. His discography boasts two albums. *Cheese* (2010) put him on the map, and *Racine Carrée* (2013) looks as though it will keep him there.

85

Note: The name "Stromae" is **verlan,** a form of French slang that inverts syllables and plays around with the language to create new words. When you flip "stro" and "mae", you get "maestro", et voila! It is kind of like Pig Latin taken to a whole new level of fun, huh? Do not worry – we will be seeing more of this very soon.

L'Activité du Jour: Activity of the Day

Lire un Livre: Read a book

Reading a book in another language does not have to be saved until you become fluent. There are plenty of books that are not of the *See Spot Run* variety that you can start reading now, and future fluent-you will thank you for it.

That does not mean it is going to be a breezy read-through, though. For this exercise, you must have a dictionary on-hand, and you will be reading from it often. As you go along, you will pick up grammar constructions and solidify what you have already learned. Take your time, do not get discouraged, and know that your mind is soaking it all in. It sure beats the French version of *See Spot Run*. I guarantee it.

There are plenty of options to choose from, but today we will stick with two recommendations:

Albert Camus – *L'Étranger* (1942)

This French Nobel Prize-winning author is the father of absurdism, a post-WWII art movement characterized by gleaning meaning from the nonsensical. In this way, L'Étranger is a unique glimpse into the collective consciousness of a world horrified and confused by the ravages of a world war. Meursault, a French Algerian and the novel's main character, kicks the novel into high gear after he commits a grievous crime directly following his mother's funeral. The novel is divided into two parts, detailing Muersault's mind frame in first-person before and after the murder. Camus summed up the novel himself, saying:

"In our society, any man who does not weep at his mother's funeral runs the risk of being sentenced to death."

With a summary like that, you know you are in for quite a ride. This novel makes the recommendation list for its simple and easy-to-understand narrative style. The themes are looming and large with this pick, but you will be able to ponder them without scratching your head over the language more than you need to.

Marguerite Duras – *L'Amante Anglaise* (1967)

Marguerite Duras is one of the nation's foremost feminist writers. Born in French Indochina (now Vietnam) in 1914, she made her way to her family's native-country, France, and remained there until her death. Although some of her earlier works do not quite fit the genre, she is often associated with the rule-breaking nouveau roman (new novel) movement of the 1950's.

In *L'Amante Anglaise*, we see her tackle a crime novel about the grisly murder of a small-town woman. Each chapter details the interrogation of a new witness, and it becomes very clear early on that each individual is unreliable or untrustworthy. Since it is wholly comprised of dialogue set up in an interview format, it is incredibly easy to understand. It is also a well-crafted treatise on gender identity and mental illness, and the mystery itself unfolds with equal depth. Even the title, "The English Lover," is a play on words. "La mente anglaise" (English mint) is a huge symbol in the novel, and it is this duality, even in the title, that makes this such an intriguing read.

À demain! (See you tomorrow!)

Chapter 6 – Day 6
Très Chic: Shopping and Urban Culture

Today, we will touch on the French nasal vowels, fashion, shopping, asking questions, and popular culture.

La Prononciation - Pronunciation: The Finishing Touch: French Nasal Vowels

The French nasal vowels are the last in our series of pesky French sounds. These are **AN, IN, ON**, and **UN**, respectively. The great thing about nasal vowels is that they are present in English as well, so they will not be as foreign as "U" or "R."

Unlike French oral vowels, which are produced within the mouth, French nasal vowels are produced using both the mouth and nose. We see this in English with words/colloquialisms like *sing, huh,* and *own*. English does not have an official distinction between nasal and oral vowels like French does, but we do unconsciously employ similar sounds.

In French, nasal vowels are generally followed by **n** or **m**, and it is in these two letters that most of the challenge lies. Their only purpose is to act as signifiers that the vowel or vowel combination preceding them should be nasalized, so this means they are not pronounced. This can cause a mess of confusion for English-speakers who take this to mean that the language "cuts off" the end of words, especially due to the fact that English does the exact opposite in relation to nasal vowels. A better way to look at it is to view **n** and **m** as nifty pronunciation cues, ensuring that you pronounce the word with that iconic nasal twang.

First, it is necessary to recognize what a nasal vowel feels like in English. Place a finger along the side of your nose and say "mmm." Notice the vibration? This indicates that you are making this sound nasally. Now keep your finger along your nose and elongate the **s** sound, just like you are mimicking a snake. This is pronounced orally, so we do not feel this vibration. This is the key to making sure you are pronouncing French nasal vowels correctly.

With this information, getting the hang of nasal vowels is as simple as learning the essence of each sound.

The Nasal A – AN

The nasal "A" is pronounced like **ahn**, where the **n** represents the nasal sound. It is pronounced by keeping the lips unrounded and nasalizing the oral "A" vowel. Remember that nasalizing means pronouncing through both your nose and mouth. It is most commonly spelled as the following (remember that they will all be pronounced the same):

- an
- am
- en

Examples:

Listen Track 80:

an – year	France – France
enfant – child	chambre – room
grand – big, tall	emmener – to take

The Nasal I – IN

The nasal "I" sound sounds like **en**, where the **n** represents the nasal sound. It is most commonly spelled with:

- in
- ain
- ein
- un

Examples:

Listen Track 81:

un – a, one	dessein – aim
bain – bath	cinq – five
pain – bread	peinture – painting

The Nasal O – ON

The nasal "O" sounds like **on**, where the **n** indicates nasalization. It is pronounced by nasalizing the close "O" vowel. Spellings include:

- on
- om

Examples:

Listen Track 82:

on – we	accompli – accomplished
bon – good	bonbon – candy
plomb – lead	bonjour – hello

The Nasal U – UN

Although this sound is rapidly becoming defunct with younger generations and is absent in certain dialects, it has not completely disappeared. It sounds like **euhn**, where the **n** indicates nasalization. It is pronounced by nasalizing the open **eu** vowel combination. For those looking to follow the younger generation's trend, pronounce this sound the same as **IN**. It is generally spelled as:

- un
- um

Examples:

Listen Track 83:

parfum – perfume	brun – brown
lundi – Monday	commun – common, ordinary

Le Vocabulaire - Vocabulary: The Art of a Good Deal: French Shopping Vocabulary

There is a good chance you will be taking advantage of being in one of the fashion capitals of the world, and that is where shopping vocabulary comes in handy. Whether you are snatching up some bargains for yourself or searching for the perfect gift, these terms will help you get what you need and know how to pay for it.

0 – zéro	16 – seize	90 – quatre-vingt-dix
1 – un	17 – dix-sept	100 – cent
2 – deux	18 – dix-huit	125 – cent vingt-cinq
3 – trois	19 – dix-neuf	200 – deux cent
4 – quatre	20 – vingt	300 – trois cent
5 – cinq	21 – vingt et un	400 – quatre cent
6 – six	22 – vingt-deux	500 – cinq cent
7 – sept	23 – vingt-trois	600 – six cent
8 – huit	24 – vingt-quatre	700 – sept cent
9 – neuf	25 – vingt-cinq	800 – huit cent
10 – dix	30 – trente	900 – neuf cent
11 – onze	40 – quarante	999 – neuf cent quatre-vingt-dix- neuf
12 – douze	50 – cinquante	1000 – mille
13 – treize	60 – soixante	
14 – quatorze	70 – soixante-dix	
15 – quinze	80 – quatre-vingts	

Numbers:

Listen Track 84:

Currency:

Listen Track 85:

l'argent – money

les espèces – cash

une carte de crédit – credit card

une carte bancaire, une carte bleue – debit card

un chèque – check

un chéquier – checkbook

la monnaie – change

une carte cadeau – gift card

le compte bancaire – bank account

le solde bancaire – bank balance

le distributeur automatique, le distributeur – ATM

Clothing:

Listen Track 86:

des vêtements – clothes

une chemise – shirt

un chemisier – blouse

une chemise à manches longues – long-sleeved shirt

une chemise à manches courtes – short-sleeved shirt

un haut – top

un pull, un sweat – sweater

un tee-shirt – tee-shirt

une jupe – skirt

une jupe droite – pencil skirt

une robe – dress

une robe d'été – sundress

une tenue de soirée – evening gown

une robe de mariée – wedding gown

un pantalon – pants

un jean – jeans

un jean moulant – skinny jeans

un jean évasé – boot-cut jeans

un jean à pattes d'éléphant – flared jeans

un jean taille basse – low-rise jeans

un short – shorts

un survêtement, un survêt – tracksuit

un bas de survêtement – track pants

un pantalon de yoga – yoga pants

un manteau – coat

une parka – parka

une veste – jacket

un costume – suit

un costume sur mesure – tailored suit

des boutons de manchette – cufflinks

un chapeau – hat

un fedora – fedora

une cravate – tie

une montre – watch

un collant – tights

un legging – leggings

des chaussettes – socks

des mi-bas – knee socks

des sous-vêtements – underwear

un caleçon – boxers

une culotte, une petite culotte – panties

un soutien-gorge – bra

un soutien-gorge push-up – push-up bra

une brassière de sport – sports bra

une robe de chambre – nightgown

un pyjama – pajamas

Shoes:

Listen Track 87:

des chaussures – shoes

des baskets, des tennis – sneakers, tennis shoes

des chaussures de randonnée – hiking boots

des chaussures de ville – oxfords

des chaussures plates – flats

des ballerines – ballerina flats

des tongs, des nu-pieds – flip-flops

des sandales – sandals

des talons hauts, des chaussures à talon – high heels

des escapins – stilettos

des espadrilles – espadrilles

des bottes – boots

des bottes à talon – high-heel boots

des bottines – ankle boots

des bottes de pluie – rain boots

des après-ski – snow boots

Materials:

Listen Track 88:

acrylique – acrylic

de coton – cotton

en cuir – leather

de daim – suede

de feutre – felt

en laine – woolen

de nylon – nylon

en polyester – polyester

en soie – silk

de tissu synthétique – synthetic

Sizing:

Listen Track 89:

une taille – size

prendre les mensurations – to take measurements

une petite taille – small

une taille moyenne – medium

une grande taille – large

les petites tailles – petite (section)

de grande taille – plus-size

une taille d'échantillon – sample size

une pointure – shoe size

un bonnet (a, b, c, d, etc.) – bra size

un tour de taille – waist size

un tour de hanches – hip size

une cabine d'essayage – fitting room

La Grammaire – Grammar: Question Everything / How to Pose Questions in French

There are four ways to ask questions in French, and all of them have a different feel. Some are formal, while others are casual and breezy. The best part is they are all exceedingly easy to master, so the question possibilities are truly endless.

1. **Est-ce que...**

Remember **Est-ce que** from yesterday? Well, it is back today, ready to magically turn any statement into a question. Simply add it to the beginning of a sentence, and **voilà** (there you have it)! Note that this form is considered more informal.

Examples:

Listen Track 90:

Est-ce que vous aimez les chats? Do you like cats?

Est-ce que c'est possible d'avoir cette boisson avec des glaçons? Is it possible to have this drink on the rocks?

Est-ce que tu as un plan? Do you have a map?

You can even add **qui** (who), **quel/quelle** (which), **quand** (when), and **pourquoi** (why) to help specify the question. Just add one of these words prior to **est-ce que**.

Examples:

Qui est-ce que tu aimes? Whom do you love?

Quelle partie est-ce que tu préfères? Which section do you prefer?

Quand est-ce qu'il y a une projection pour ce film? When is there a showing for this film?

Pourquoi est-ce qu'elle toujours si énergique? Why is she always so energetic?

2. **Inflectional Questions**

Another super easy and informal way to ask a question is by ending any statement with an interrogative inflection, or raised pitch. This is nearly universal with questions in English, so this should be a piece of cake.

Examples:

Listen Track 91:

Vous aimez ce film? You like this movie?

Tu veux faire une promenade? You wanna take a walk?

Il est en retard? He's late?

Nous n'achetons pas encore les billets? We didn't buy the tickets yet?

Elle n'aime pas le rap? She doesn't like rap?

3. N'est-ce pas

By adding a comma and **n'est-ce pas** (literally translated as *is it not*) to the end of a sentence, you have just created another informal question. Note that this is the rough equivalent of saying *right?* in English when you are assuming someone will agree with you, so it is paired with an affirmative statement.

Examples:

Listen Track 92:

Tu nages, n'est-ce pas? You swim, right?

Il est beau, n'est-ce pas? He's handsome, isn't he?

Nous sommes à l'heure, n'est-ce pas? We're on time, right?

4. Inversion

The most difficult of the interrogative forms, this is the form where you flip the conjugated verb and subject pronoun. It is always, always, always paired with a hyphen. Note that this is the most formal of the interrogative forms.

Examples:

Listen Track 93:

Chantez-vous? Do you sing?

As-tu un potager? Do you have a vegetable garden?

Veux-tu faire les courses? Do you want to go shopping?

Just like **est-ce que**, you can use inversion to ask negative questions. Simply add **ne** and **pas** around the inversion.

Examples:

Listen Track 94:

N'aimez-vous pas cette couleur? Don't you like this color?

Ne chantez-vous pas? Don't you sing?

Ne sont-ils pas encore arrivés? Haven't they arrived yet?

You can also add words like **qui, quand, quel/quelle**, and **pourquoi** at the beginning of a sentence, just like **est-ce que**:

Examples:

Listen Track 95:

Qui est-elle? Who is she?

Quand veux-tu aller au cinéma? When do you want to go to the movie theater?

Quel vol choisissez-vous? Which flight did you choose?

Pourquoi aimes-tu cette robe? Why do you like this dress?

When inversion creates two vowels next to one another, you must add -t- between them.

Examples:

Aime-t-il les romans policiers? Does he like crime novels?

Travaille-t-elle à la boulangerie? Does she work at the bakery?

Si: Responding Affirmatively to a Negative Question

Unlike English, French has a way to respond to a negative question with "yes, I am" using one word. Simply use **si**! **Oui** is reserved for affirmative questions.

Examples:

Listen Track 96:

Ne vas-tu pas au concert? You're not going to the concert?

Si! Yes, I am!

Est-ce que tu ne fais pas du jogging? Don't you go jogging?

Si, je le fais chaque matin. Yes, I do it every morning.

Vous n'aimez pas ces affiches? You don't like these posters?

Si, je les aime beaucoup. Yes, I like them a lot.

La Conversation – Speaking: Shop 'Till You Drop / Making Purchases in French

Navigating shops, finding the right size, and cash-handling can all seem dizzying in a foreign language. This section is filled with useful exchanges you will encounter as you shop. With the right phrases, there is no need to try and figure it out on your own.

While Shopping:

Listen Track 97:

Avez-vous… – Do you have…

Où puis-je trouver... – Where can I find…

Je regarde, c'est tout. – I'm just looking.

Je cherche un chemisier beige. – I'm looking for a beige blouse.

Où sont les cabines d'essayages? - Where are the fitting rooms?

Combien ça coute? – How much does this cost?

Je peux l'essayer? – Can I try it on?

Vous l'avez en une taille moyenne? – Do you have it in a size medium?

C'est trop petit/grand. – It's too small/large.

À quelle heure est-ce que vous ouvrez/fermez? – At what time do you open/close?

Puis-je retourner cet article? – May I return this item?

Cashing Out:

Listen Track 98:

Je voudrais payer par carte de crédit. – I would like to pay by credit card.

C'est un cadeau. Pourriez-vous me l'emballer, s'il vous plait? – It's a gift. Could you gift-wrap it for me, please?

Je voudrais un reçu. – I would like a receipt.

Acceptez-vous… – Do you accept…

Nous n'accepterons pas les cartes de crédit. – We don't accept credit cards.

Tapez votre code secret ici. – Enter your pin number here.

Valider – Accept

Annuler – Cancel

Retrait? – Withdrawl funds? (Option at electronic pay terminals)

Choisir un montant. – Choose an amount.

Signez ici. – Sign here.

Souhaitez-vous un recu? – Would you like a receipt?

L'Immersion – Immersion: Getting with the Program: Cultural Trends and "Verlan"

Le Film du Jour: Film of the Day

"Persepolis"

Persepolis might ring a bell for you. It was nominated for Best Animated Feature at the 80th Academy Awards, and *Time* rated it one of the top ten films of 2007. The accolades multiply in number when we turn our attention to France. The film was heralded as a cinematic masterpiece and a modern take on contemporary French culture.

Adapted from a comic of the same name, the film itself is animated, but do not let that fool you. The plot touches on political upheaval, revolution, and violence. Set against the backdrop of the 1970's Iranian Revolution, this autobiographical tale weaves the coming-of-age story of a headstrong young girl who becomes a counter-cultural modern woman. While it stands as a unique history lesson for those unfamiliar with Iranian history, it also stands as a testament to the diverse cultural representations present in French culture. Startling and cheeky all at once, this film is an informative enchantment.

La Musique du Jour: Music of the Day

Jeanne Cherhal

2015 has been good to Jeanne Cherhal. Her most recent album landed her as a contender for "Best Female Artist" at the 2015 Victoire de la Musique (the French version of the Grammy's). Shortly before that, she was named a **chevalier** (knight) by the French Minister of Culture, which is a pretty big deal. It has been a slow-build, but Cherhal has worked her way into the highest echelons of French music culture, just like the greats that influence her iconic sound. Cherhal is firmly rooted in the **nouvelle chanson** (new song) movement, which is characterized by vocals and instrumentals reminiscent of old-school French songwriters. What puts the "nouvelle" in "nouvelle chanson" is witty, wry lyrics full of theatricality and spunk. This genre produces ballads for modern France, and this is where Cherhal has had so much success. Her captivating live performances are filled with refreshing takes on French cabaret à la Regina Spektor.

Her debut album, *Jeanne Cherhal* (2001), has a decidedly Edith Piaf-esque sound. *Douze Fois par An* (2004) picked up the Victoire la Musique for Best New Artist. With *L'eau* (2006) and *Charade* (2007), she experiments with avant-garde to great effect. And, finally, *Historie de J* (2014) is her latest offering, which harkens back to her earlier focus on retro influences. It is definitely worth a listen. "Quand c'est non, c'est non" is a great place to start.

L'Activité du Jour: Activity of the Day

Jouer avec le Verlan: Play with Verlan

Yesterday, we touched briefly on Stromae's name being an excellent example of **verlan**, which you will remember is the inversion of syllables to create new French words. Not only is it a great way to recognize patterns and pronunciation in French words, it is also a fun way to show a heightened level of mastery of the French language. Unlike pig Latin, which really is not widely used in English, certain verlan words have become a part of the everyday ins and outs of the French language. Because of this, our goal today is to play around with verlan to create our own words and learn some of the staples. So, whip out some paper and a pen and **zyva** (or **vas-y**, meaning *go*)!

The easiest way to verlan a word is to:

1. Separate the syllables
2. Reverse the syllables
3. Put the word back together
4. Eradicate any unnecessary letters
5. Add/change letters as needed

To ensure that the word reflects its pronunciation, verlaned words are often tweaked. This usually means that some letters are dropped and replaced with letters that make more sense pronunciation-wise. There really is not much of a rhyme or reason to this, so it is either based on the established verlan or, in the case of you creating your own, your own creativity.

"Verlan" itself is a verlan of **l'envers**, or *reverse*, so let's try creating it:

Original: l'envers

Separate: l'en...vers

Flip: vers...l'en

Combine: versl'en

Simplify: verslen

Eradicate: verlen

Finish: verlan

As you can see, verlan ends up being a word puzzle of sorts. Let's try another:

Original: sortir (to leave)

Separate: sor...tir

Flip: tir...sor

Combine: tirsor

Finish: tirsor

Note that **tirsor** did not need any additional changes due to its pronunciation flowing well.

Now for today's activity! Look through your French dictionary and find some words that speak to you. Try your hand at turning these into verlan. It is not about making it perfect, so get creative and have fun with it. This exercise is a great way to really get you focusing on phonetics and diction without having to whip out a dry, boring textbook. Becoming comfortable with a language involves a lot of toying around with it until it is not so intimidating anymore, and verlan exaggerates what our brains naturally do to try and make sense of words and sounds.

Here are some notable examples of verlan. Since these are all slang terms, it goes without saying that you can use them at your own discretion. In the right situation, they are **super looc** (*super cool*, that is).

French Verlan:

Listen Track 99:

balpeau – verlan of "peau de balle"

meaning: nothing, zip

barjot – verlan of "jobard"

meaning: crazy, insane

une cecla – verlan of "une classe"

meaning: class

céfran – verlan of "français"

meaning: French

chanmé – verlan of "méchant"

meaning: mean, nasty

chébran – verlan of "branché"

meaning: cool, plugged in

chelou – verlan of "louche"

meaning: shady, dubious

un skeud – verlan of "un disque"

meaning: record, album

fais ièche – verlan of "fais chier"

meaning: it's boring, annoying

geudin – verlan of "dingue"

meaning: crazy

un kebla – verlan of "un Black" (from English)

meaning: black person

kéblo – verlan of "bloqué"

meaning: blocked, caught

un keuf (now *feuk*) – verlan of "un flic"

meaning: police officer (equivalent to cop, copper, pig)

un keum – verlan of "un mec"

meaning: guy, dude

laisse béton – verlan of "laisse tomber"

meaning: forget it, drop it

une meuf – verlan of "une femme"

meaning: woman, wife

ouf – verlan of "fou"

meaning: crazy

pécho – verlan of "une chopper"

meaning: to steal; to get caught

le pera – verlan of "le rap"

meaning: rap (music)

relou – verlan of "lourd"

meaning: heavy

un reuf – verlan of "un frère"

meaning: brother

une reum – verlan of "une mère"

meaning: mother

un reup – verlan of "un père"

meaning: father

une reus – verlan of "une sœur"

meaning: sister

ripou – verlan of "pourri"

meaning: rotten, corrupt

la siquemu / la sicmu /zikmu – verlan of "la musique"

meaning: music

une teuf – verlan of "une fête"

meaning: party

une tof – verlan of "une photo"

meaning: photograph

le tromé – verlan of "le metro"

meaning: subway

zarbi – verlan of "bizarre"

meaning: strange

À plus! (See you later!)

Chapter 7 – Day 7
Bon Voyage: Traveling

Our last day will be all about polishing up and refining what we have learned. We will touch on French tongue twisters, verb conjugation, vacation terms, and personalizing your learning experience.

La Prononciation: Pronunciation - Getting Tongue-Tied: French Virelangues (Tongue Twisters)

You've done it! After conquering all the common pronunciation pitfalls present in French, it is time to kick it up one last notch. Yes, that means French tongue twisters, otherwise known as "**les virelangues.**" Practicing tongue twisters is a great way to refine and reinforce all that you have learned. They also act as another method for learning new vocabulary and phrases that can be used in conversation.

Just like in English, French native speakers try to say these as fast as possible. This is not our aim for today's lesson. Especially since these virelangues are difficult to master even for native speakers, your goal will be to approach these with intentionality, not speed. Getting familiar with pronouncing whole virelangues will take time and patience, so try to focus on pronouncing each word separately before pairing them together. Once you feel comfortable reading the whole virelangue, try to isolate difficult areas and repeat them until it feels more natural. Finally, once you are able to read the virelangue without mistakes, practice repeating it over and over again, slowly building speed. Before you know it, you will be the next virelangue champion!

Here are ten famous ones to get you started:

Les Virelangues: French Tongue Twisters

Listen Track 100:

1. **Cinq chiens chassent six chats.**

   Five dogs are chasing six cats.

2. **Le mur murant Paris rend Paris murmurant.**

   The wall walling Paris drives Paris to murmuring.

3. **Les chaussettes de l'archiduchesse sont-elles sèches ? Archi-sèches!**

   Are the socks of the archduchess dry? Very dry!

4. **Si mon tonton tond ton tonton, ton tonton tondu sera!**

   If my uncle shaves your uncle, your uncle will be shaved!

5. **Fruits frais, fruits frits, fruits cuits, fruits crus.**

   Fresh fruit, fried fruit, cooked fruit, raw fruit.

6. **As-tu vu le vert ver allant vers le verre en verre vert?**

   Did you see the green worm going towards the green glass?

7. **Didon dîna, dit-on, du dos dodu d'un dodu dindon.**

   Dido dined, they say, from the plump back of a plump turkey.

8. **Un chasseur sachant chasser sait chasser sans son chien de chasse.**

   A hunter who knows how to hunt knows how to hunt without his hunting dog.

9. **Cinq gros rats grillent dans la grosse graisse grasse.**

   Five fat rats grill in the big, fatty fat.

10. **Ces six saucissons-secs-ci sont si secs qu'on ne sait si s'en sont.**

    These six dried sausages are so dry that we don't know if they are (sausages).

Le Vocabulaire: Vocabulary - Wanderlust Defined: French Vacation Vocabulary

The ultimate reason to learn vocabulary is so that you will be able to communicate and comprehend with confidence. Because of this, we will be focusing on in-country travel and vacation vocabulary. Whether you are traveling to France for business or pleasure, this vocab paired with what you have already learned will make it so that you will be able to get where you need to go…and chat about it along the way!

At the Airport:

Listen Track 101:

un avion – airplane

un vol – flight

une porte – gate

une compagnie aérienne – airline

les billets d'avion – airplane tickets

un aller simple – one-way ticket

un billet aller-retour – round-trip ticket

une carte d'embarquement – boarding pass

la classe économique, la classe eco (informal) – coach (economy) lass

la première classe – first class

une hôtesse, un steward, un membre d'équipage – flight attendant (female, male, male or female)

l'enregistrement – check-in

les bagages à main – carry-on luggage

un bagage à main, un bagage cabine (informal) – carry-on bag

les bagages enregistrés – checked luggage

un bagage en soute – checked bag

le retrait de bagages – baggage claim

le contrôle de sécurité – security check

la douane – customs

les documents de voyage – travel documents

les exigences d'immunisation – immunization requirements

les frais de voyage – travel costs

le passeport – passport

le visa – visa

remplir les formulaires – to fill out forms

renouveler un passeport – to renew a passport

se procurer les documents de voyage – to obtain travel documents

Activities:

Listen Track 102:

faire un voyage – to go on a trip

aller en vacances – to go on vacation

faire du tourisme – to go sightseeing

voyager – to tour, to go on a tour

loger – to stay (at a hotel)

se loger – to find accommodation

faire une excursion – to go on an excursion

flâner – to wander, stroll

lire – to read

pique-niquer – to go on a picnic

jouer – to play (sports, etc.)

faire du vélo – to go for a bike ride

aller à la plage – to go to the beach

nager – to go swimming

naviguer – to go boating

faire du surf – to go surfing

faire du ski – to go skiing

faire du snowboard, faire du surf des neiges – to go snowboarding

faire du patin à glace – to go ice skating

monter, grimper – to climb

faire du camping – to go camping

faire de la randonnée – to go hiking

faire de l'escalade – to go rock-climbing

Geographic Locations:

Listen Track 103:

la plage – the beach

une île – island

une rivière, un fleuve – river

une mare – pond

un lac – lake

le bois – forest

la campagne – countryside

une montagne – mountain

le sommet – summit

le pic – peak

une chaine de montagnes – mountain chain

une colline – hill

une vallée – valley

un vignoble – vineyard

la région viticole – wine country

une ville – town, city

le centre-ville – downtown

un monument – monument

une statue – statue

un lieu historique – historic site

un site touristique – touristic site

La Grammaire - Grammar: And...Action!: Foolproof Tips for Present-Tense Verb Conjugation

It is difficult to discuss anything in a foreign language without having a good grasp of verb conjugation. French language-learners tend to get overwhelmed by the idea of having to conjugate based on the pronoun for each and every verb, but it is actually simpler than it seems. So simple, in fact, that it is possible to master nearly all French verbs just by knowing three different sets of endings.

Why? Well, there are these wonderful things in French called **les verbes réguliers** (regular verbs). They are called regular verbs because they share the same standard endings with other verbs. There are three sets of regular verbs in French: -**ER**, -**IR**, and -**RE**. Once you know to conjugate with je/te/il,elle/nous/vous/ils for just *one* -**ER** verb, you know all of the conjugations for all of the -**ER** verbs. The same goes for -**IR** and -**RE**. Again, these three sets make up most of the verbs you will find in the French language, so it becomes exceedingly easy to gain a lot of grammar ground in a very short period of time.

Before we look at each set of conjugations, we will reinforce how the present tense is used in French.

Le Présent – Present Tense

The French present tense resembles English quite closely. It is used to express:

11. Current Actions

Example:

Je lis. I am reading.

Habitual Actions

Example:

Je joue au football chaque samedi.

I play soccer every Saturday.

12. If/Then Conditional Statements

Example:

Si je vais au supermarché, j'achèterai des bonbons. If I go to the supermarket, I will buy candy.

Note: The conjugation **achèterai**, or *will buy*, is part of **le futur** (the future tense).

13. Absolute Truths and General Statements

Example:

La vie continue. Life goes on.

En Train De...

One of the biggest differences between French and English present tenses is that French does not have helping verbs, as in "I am eating." This means that a phrase like **Je dors** can mean "I am sleeping," "I sleep," or "I do sleep." If you want to specify that you are in the middle of doing something, you can use this formula:

JE SUIS + EN TRAIN DE + VERB INFINITIVE

Example:

Je suis en train d'étudier. I am in the process of studying.

This formula is not as common as just conjugating the verb and gathering the implied meaning, but it is useful when you need to make sure someone knows something is happening at that moment.

Now we will move on to learning **how to conjugate each verb set.**

"-ER" Verbs

To conjugate regular **-ER** verbs in the present tense, all you have to do is remove the infinitive ending (in this case, **-ER**) and add on the standard endings. They are:

Je – e	Nous – ons
Tu – es	Vous – ez
Il/elle – e	Ils/elles – ent

Simple, right? Now we can use this guide for any regular -ER verb. Here are some examples:

Danser: to dance

dans-

Listen Track 104:

Je danse	Nous dansons
Tu danses	Vous dansez
Il/elle danse	Ils/elles dansent

Penser: to think

pens-

Listen Track 105:

Je pense	Nous pensons
Tu penses	Vous pensez
Il/elle pense	Ils/elles pensent

Écouter: to listen

écout-

Listen Track 106:

J'écoute	Nous écoutons
Tu écoutes	Vous écoutez
Il/elle écoute	Ils/elles écoutent

"-IR" Verbs

With regular **-IR** verbs, you cut off the infinitive ending (in this case, **-IR**) and add the standard **-IR** conjugations. They are:

Je – is	Nous – issons
Tu – is	Vous – issez
Il/elle – it	Ils/elles – issent

Here are some examples of common -IR verbs:

Choisir: to choose

chois-

Listen Track 107:

Je choisis	Nous choisissons
Tu choisis	Vous choisissez
Il/elle choisit	Ils/elles choisissent

Agir: to act

ag-

Listen Track 108:

J'agis	Nous agissons
Tu agis	Vous agissez
Il/elle agit	Ils/elles agissent

Finir: to finish **fin-**

Listen Track 109:

Je finis	Nous finissons
Tu finis	Vous finissez
Il/elle finit	Ils/elles finissent

"-RE" Verbs

To conjugate regular **-RE** verbs, drop the infinitive ending (in this case, **-RE**) and add the regular **-IR** endings. They are:

Je – s	Nous – ons
Tu – s	Vous – ez
Il/elle – (nothing)	Ils/elles – ent

Here are some common **-RE** verbs:

Attendre: to wait

attend-

Listen Track 110:

J'attends	Nous attendons
Tu attends	Vous attendez
Il/elle attend	Ils/ells attendent

Répondre: to respond

répond-

Listen Track 111:

Je réponds	Nous répondons
Tu réponds	Vous répondez
Il/elle répond	Ils/ells répondent

Rendre: to give back, return

rend-

Listen Track 112:

Je rends	Nous rendons
Tu rends	Vous rendez
Il/elle rend	Ils/elles rendent

How easy is that? Now you can literally conjugate hundreds of French verbs with ease. Regular -**ER, -IR,** and -**RE** verbs each have their own standard endings when conjugating in passé compose, imparfait, and the le futur as well, so it is as simple as following this same procedure with the other tenses.

La Conversation – Speaking: Getting Around: Taxi Travel and Hotel Terms

Knowing how to get where you need to go and securing lodging are two of the most important things to learn in a foreign language. Taxi travel, especially in Paris, can be difficult to secure, so it is important to have phrases to give you a leg up. As for lodging, being able to ask the questions that need to be asked can mean the difference between being comfortable during your stay and letting your hotel detract from your travel experience.

These phrases will enable you to navigate taxi travel and get the most out of your hotel.

Taking a Taxi:

Listen Track 113:

Est-ce qu'il y a un bon endroit pour héler un taxi près d'ici? – Is there a good place to hail a taxi near here?

Y a-t-il une station de taxi près de l'aéroport? – Is there a taxi station near the airport?

Pouvez-vous m'appeler un taxi, s'il vous plait? – Could you call a taxi for me, please?

Pouvez-vous envoyer un taxi à... – Could you send a taxi to…

Pouvez-vous m'aider avec mes bagages, s'il vous plait? – Could you help me with my bags, please?

Je voudrais aller à... – I would like to go to…

Pouvez-vous me conduire à... – Could you drive me to…

Combien ça coûte pour aller à... – How much does it cost to go to…

C'est près d'ici? – Is it near here?

C'est tout près. – It's very close.

C'est assez loin. – It's quite far.

Arrêtez-vous ici, s'il vous plait. – Stop here, please.

Je descends ici. – I'll get off here.

À quel point est-ce que le prix de la course augmente? – At what point does the fare go up?

At the Hotel:

Listen Track 114:

Avez-vous des chambres disponibles? – Do you have any rooms available?

Pouvez-vous me suggérer un autre hôtel près d'ici? – Could you suggest another hotel nearby?

J'ai fait une réservation au nom de… – I made a reservation under the name…

Je voudrais une chambre pour trois nuits avec un grand lit. – I would like a room for three nights with a double bed.

À quelle heure dois-je libérer ma chambre? – At what time do I need to check-out of my room?

Avez-vous quelque chose de moins chère? – Do you have anything less expensive?

Où est-ce que vous servez le petit déjeuner? – Where do you serve breakfast?

Je voudrais libérer ma chambre. – I would like to check-out.

Où se trouve la piscine? – Where is the swimming pool?

Est-ce qu'il y a un coffre-fort dans ma chambre? – Is there a safe in my room?

J'ai besoin de/d'… – I need…

-un oreiller – a pillow

-une couverture en plus – another blanket

-un savon – soap

-papier toilette – toilet paper

Votre chambre est sur… – Your room is on…

-**le rez-de-chaussée** – the ground floor

-**le premier étage** – the first floor

-**le deuxième étage** – the second floor

-**le troisième étage** – the third floor

-**le   quatrième   étage** – the   fourth   floor
Vous êtes dans la chambre vingt-cinq. – You're in room 25.

Pourriez-vous me réveiller par téléphone à 8 heures du matin? – Could you give me a wake-up call at 8 in the morning?

L'Immersion – Immersion: Now It's Personal: French Comedy, Rock, and Journal Writing

Le Film du Jour: Film of the Day

"OSS 117: Cairo, Nest of Spies (OSS 117: Le Caire, nid d'espions)"

OSS 117: Cairo, Nest of Spies, or *OSS 117: Le Caire, nid d'espions* in French, has a lot to offer English-speakers. Modeled after Jean Bruce's novels and subsequent spy films of the 1950's and 1960's, this modern (and humorous) take on the spy film genre feels a lot like the James Bond films English-speakers know and love. There is also the fact that you might recognize Jean Dujardin and Bérénice Bejo, stars of the Academy Award-winning film *The Artist*, who play starring roles in the film. In France, *OSS 117* garnered enough praise to warrant a sequel, *OSS 117: Lost in Rio* (*OSS 117: Rio ne répond plus*), which is also well worth a watch. Set in 1955, the film follows the hapless adventures of Hubert Bonisseur de La Bath, secret agent 117 of the Office of Strategic Services. When a fellow friend and agent disappears, OSS 117 follows the trail to Cairo, where he foils Nazi plots, stumbles around the culture, and seduces women. Since the film draws on the campiness of early spy films, Jean Dujardin speaks with enunciated clarity and panache. That means this film is a gold mine for those looking to boost their comprehension, vocabulary, and pronunciation…while laughing all along the way.

La Musique du Jour: Music of the Day

BB Brunes

And now for some rock. BB Brunes are part of "la nouvelle scène rock française," or the "new French rock scene," which pulls from punk and rock bands of the 1960's and 1970's to create a breezy, effortlessly cool sound. Their name is based on Serge Gainsbourg's song "Initial BB," and Boulevard Brune,, a neighborhood in Paris. It is a common trend among French rock bands to sing in English, so BB Brunes are often cited as one of the few French rock bands to find success singing in French. Their debut album, *Blonde Comme Moi* (2007), debuted while the band was still in high school. By the time their second album, *Nico Teen Love* (2009), was released, the band was an absolute sensation. *Nico Teen Love* quickly went platinum and won the Victorie de la Musique for "Best New Artist" later that year. 2012 brought about their best album yet, *Long Courrier*, which showcased a new level of maturity in their music. The band is currently on hiatus, but you can also check out lead singer Adrien Gallo's solo side project, *Gemini* (2014). It is every bit as good as his work with the band. For BB Brunes, give "Coups et Blessures" a shot. For Adrien Gallo, try "Crocodile."

L'Activité du Jour: Activity of the Day

Un Note d'un Journal Intime: A Diary Entry

Our final activity will take you beyond this book. Creating a journal or diary to learn another language works on multiple fronts. First, you are creating a personal connection with the language. Secondly, you are practicing how to write about things beyond "the woman is tall" and "the man eats bread", so it is a great way to graduate from the basics and upgrade your grammar and vocabulary. The best thing about writing in a journal is that it is all about you and your interests. You can write about your favorite French films, recipes you are cooking, books you are reading, or the most basic details of your day. Whether you are making a travel journal or using it to write down your thoughts and feelings, commit to it. Today marks your first entry, but the best way to make this a habit is to put yourself into it.

If you want to buy a journal and a fancy pen, go for it. If you want to stick to sheets of paper and that random pencil you have lying around, more power to you. Another recommendation is to use a journaling app like Day One or Memento, which allows you to add pictures, links to French sites and study materials, and share with social media. Even if that is not your style, it is still easy to personalize your entries. Especially if you are using this journal during your travels at some point, taping or gluing tangible memories (photos, admission tickets, map scraps, restaurant wrappers, etc.) will make this something both sustainable and special.

So, grab your dictionary and go! Years down the road, you will have these entries to remind you of the beginning of your journey with the French language.

Bonne chance! (Good luck!)

How to download the MP3

Audio download instructions

- Visit this page to download the MP3: https://www.talkinfrench.com/download-mp3-french-crash-course

- Click on the book cover. It will take you to a Dropbox folder containing the MP3 file. (If you're not familiar with what Dropbox is or how it works, don't panic, it just a storage facility.)

- Click the DOWNLOAD button in the Dropbox folder located in the upper right portion of your screen. A box may pop up asking you to sign in to Dropbox. Simply click, "No thanks, continue to download" under the sign in boxes. (If you have a Dropbox account, you can choose to save it to your own Dropbox so you have access anywhere via the internet.)

- The files you have downloaded will be saved in a .zip file. Note: This is large file. Don't try opening it until your browser tells you that it has completed the download successfully (usually a few minutes on a broadband connection but if your connection is unreliable, it could take 10 to 20 minutes).

- The files will be in your "downloads" folder unless you have changed your settings. Extract them from the folder and save them to your computer or copy to your preferred devices, *et voilà !* You can now listen to the audio anytime, anywhere.

For iPpad / iPhone owners

please go to this page for further instructions:

talkinfrench.com/instructions-for-ipad-iphone-owner

If you have any issues downloading the MP3, do not hesitate contact me at frederic@talkinfrench.com.